Anyone can learn
Watercolor
Journaling
~ yes, You!

An Easy 1-2-3 Watercolor
Technique for the Beginner

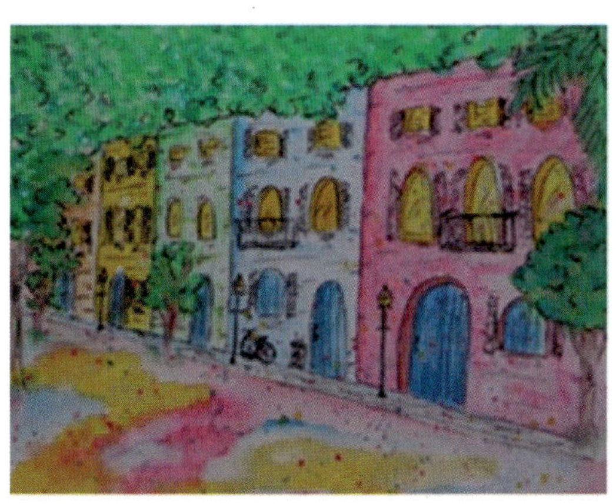

Written and
Illustrated by

Jolyn Parker

*Dedicated to my fabulous, creative,
supportive, inspiring, loving friend, Shambhavi.
Oh yeah, and silly, too.*

TABLE OF CONTENTS

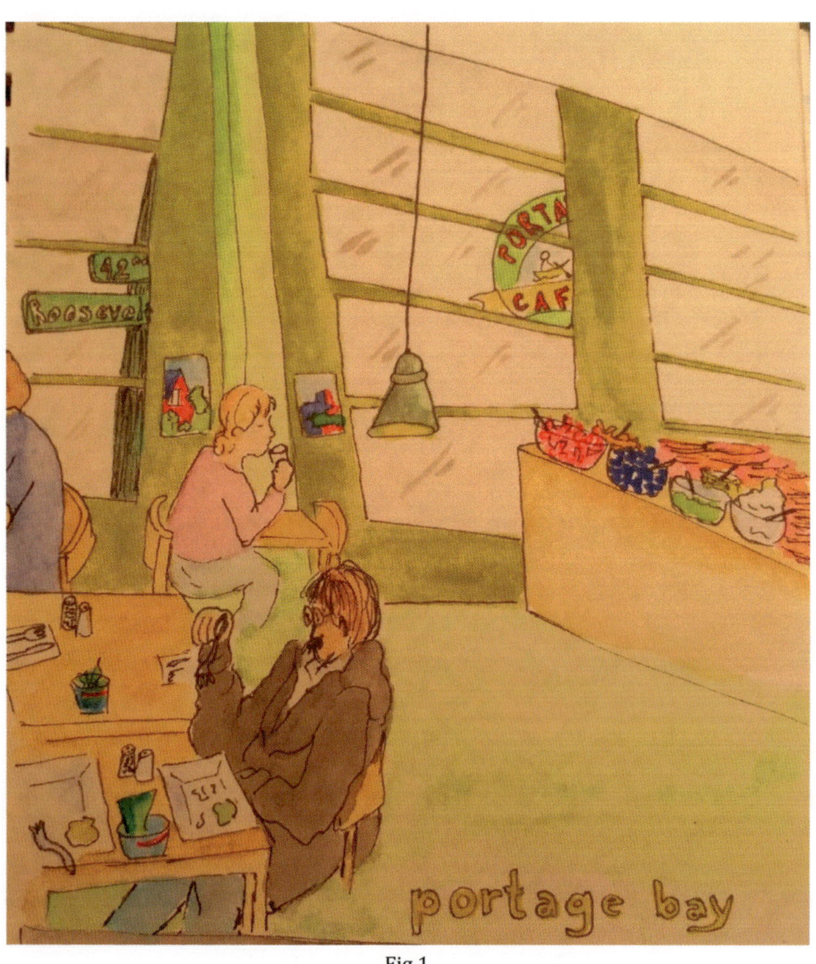

Fig.1

CHAPTER 1

ANTICIPATION

You are about to discover how easy it can be to bring your journals to life with color and simple illustrations, to capture life's moments and express your creativity through watercolor journaling.

The first response I usually get from people is, *"Oh, I can't draw,"* or the old cliché, *"Why, I couldn't draw a straight line with a ruler!"* Maybe that's your reaction, too. So let me ask you: Can you write the alphabet? Each letter is actually a picture you learned to draw as a young child even though you've always heard it called writing, not drawing. Can you draw a square? A rectangle? A triangle? Every drawing is simply some combination of curves and straight lines. If you can draw letters and simple shapes, you have all the skills you need to enjoy watercolor journaling.

"It took me four years to paint like Raphael
but a lifetime to paint like a child."
—*Pablo Picasso*

Young children are naturally creative. They love to dance when the music is lively. They will gleefully scribble color onto paper… or onto the walls when your back is turned. They sing songs they have heard and make up songs of their own. Within just a few years, unfortunately, most children have internalized the social norm that only people who are "good" at dancing or singing or drawing should do it, so most of us stopped drawing shortly after preschool. As adults we try to draw something and get frustrated because it looks like a six-year-old drew it, but that's when we stopped practicing, so our skills never progressed. Fear not!   This book will teach you an approach to sketching and watercoloring that will work even if you haven't drawn since childhood and will also advance with you as your skills grow rapidly from regular use.

In CHAPTER 2 (TOOLS OF THE TRADE) you will learn about the few, inexpensive supplies needed for watercolor journaling, where to get them and how to make them portable (and mess-free) so they are readily available whenever you have a moment to journal… on your lunch hour, as you are sightseeing, or while watching TV at night in your recliner.

CHAPTER 3 (EASY AS 1-2-3) will explain the simple approach to watercolor journaling that I have enjoyed for years. A friend introduced this technique to me in just one afternoon years ago, and I'm excited to pass it along to you so that you can experience for yourself how very simple drawings and splashes of color can add dimension and beauty to your journal.

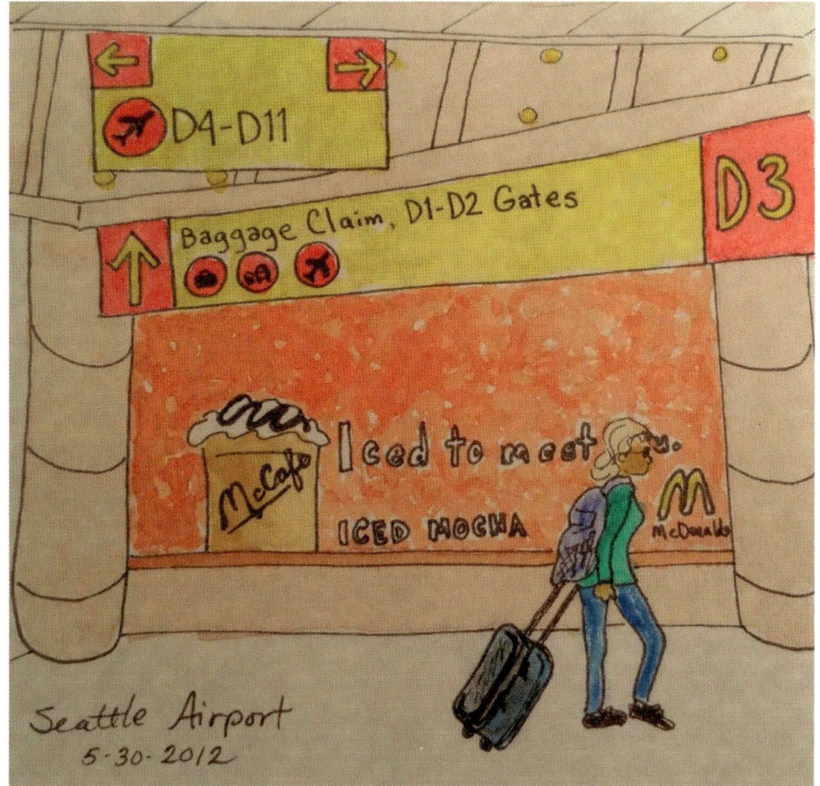

Fig.2

Anxious to get started? If you're anything like me, you don't want to spend time reading a book when you are beginning a new project, so after reading Chapters 2 and 3, you will be good to go. It really is that simple. The rest of the book, though, contains information that you may find helpful and that might add to the joy of watercolor journaling for you.

CHAPTER 4 (BECOME A SHAPE SHIFTER) is about how to find basic shapes and letters in anything you want to draw and then translate them to paper. It's so simple that if I say much more here, there won't be anything left to cover in Chapter 4. It really is an easy way to approach drawing.

As a perfectionist, I have struggled over the years to relax and appreciate my own artistic endeavors when they don't meet whatever standards I have in mind. In CHAPTER 5 (VOLUME CONTROL) you'll find ten strategies for keeping your inner critic, and the fear of not being good enough, from interfering with the joy of watercolor journaling. In fact, you just might make friends with that inner critic and teach it to give you constructive feedback.

In CHAPTER 6 (LOOKIT, LOOKIT WHAT I DID!) I'll share with you pages from a watercolor travel journal that I made on my first visit to New York City a few years ago. Taking time to sketch and watercolor at the various locations helped me soak in the ambiance and notice more details at each site, and the journal has become my favorite travel souvenir ever.

CHAPTER 7 (THE SPICE OF LIFE) will cover some simple watercolor techniques you can use to create a variety of effects in your pictures. They don't require skill so much as just knowing about them.

CHAPTER 8 (GO FOR IT!) is a call to action: Stop reading and start creating! There are also details about a chance to win a free watercolor journaling kit valued at over $50, so be sure to stick around for that.

Finally, the APPENDIX (REFERENCES) at the end of the book lists some of the books, videos and websites that I have found helpful or interesting about drawing, painting and art journaling. It is amazing how much education and inspiration is readily available on the internet, and much of it is free.

Thank you for reading this book. I am excited to see what you will create and invite you to share it with me via email.

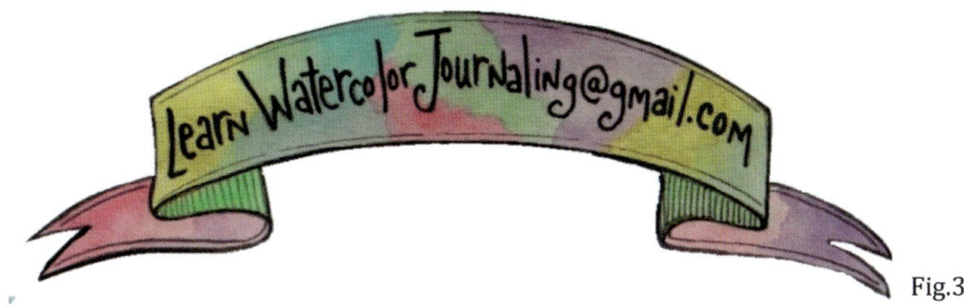

Fig.3

CHAPTER 2

TOOLS OF THE TRADE

Fortunately very few supplies are needed to do watercolor journaling, and for the most part they are quite inexpensive.

THE WATER BRUSH

I remember watercoloring in days past—walking to the kitchen sink to fill a glass with water and carrying it carefully to my painting table. I'd be ever so careful the whole time I was painting not to knock it over, but inevitably I'd spill at least a little. And then, after only a few rinses of the brush, it seemed, the water would be so muddy that I would have to carry the glass back to the kitchen, rinse it out and start all over again. Can you imagine the hassle of dealing with the water glass while sightseeing your way through New York City? Well, no more.

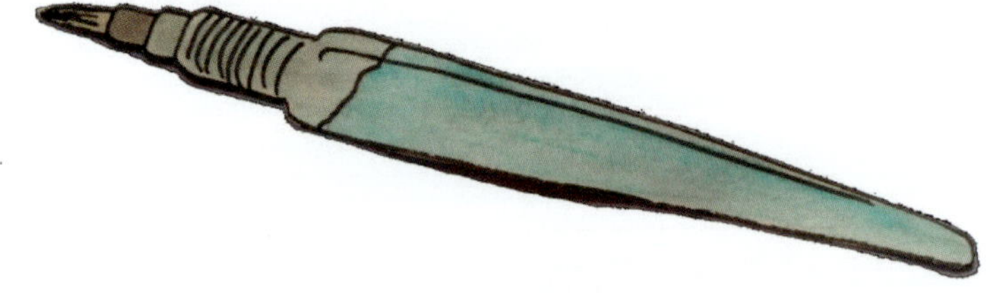

Fig.4

There's a wonderful invention called the water brush which actually has been around for quite some time but was only recently improved and is now widely available. The handle of the brush is a hollow tube that acts as a water reservoir. By squeezing very gently, water is released into the brush so it's ready to pick up the paint from your palette and apply to your picture. To dilute the paint, you simply squeeze out a bit more water. When you are ready to change colors, wipe the brush on a tissue or cloth while squeezing to release a bit of water until it runs clear. It only takes a second. Then you're ready to use your next color.

There are several brands available online and at most art supply stores, and they come with a variety of brush tips—small, medium, large, flat, slanted. Since I like to travel light, I generally just use a medium brush for everything. The only time I use the other brushes is when I'm journaling at home and have all my art supplies within easy reach.

The Tissue

Any napkin, tissue or cloth will do—whichever you prefer or have handy. I like to use a stretchy sports wrist band so I don't have to keep track of where I put the tissue or chase it in the wind. It has the added benefit of not contributing to the landfill.

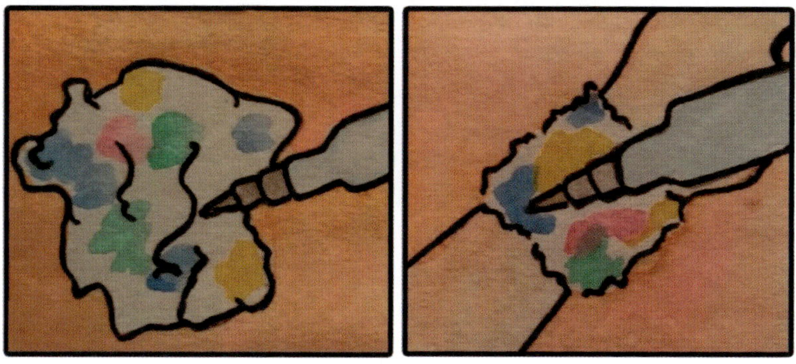

Fig.5

THE PALETTE

Any set of watercolors will do, from the cheapest palette to the fanciest. My personal favorite, though, is the Sakura Field Sketch Set because it has many colors, a mixing tray, a water brush and even a sponge in a very compact case. You can also buy the blocks of paint to refill or to change which colors you have available.

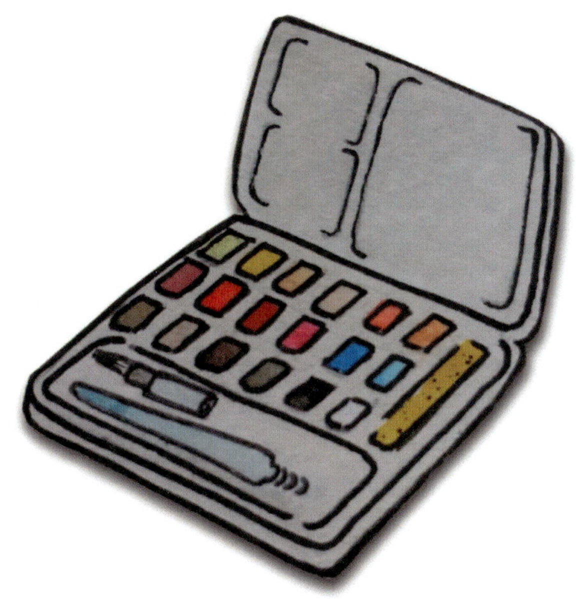

Fig.6

A good quality watercolor paper can really make a difference, both in the end product and in the ease of painting. It is more "forgiving," meaning that you can sketch with pencil, erase it and paint over the same area quite a bit without the paper showing wear. It also won't buckle and warp as much as regular paper does when it gets wet. For purposes of watercolor journaling, you'll want to have an actual watercolor journal; that is, a journal made with watercolor paper. The word "watercolor" will appear somewhere on the label if it is actually intended for that purpose.

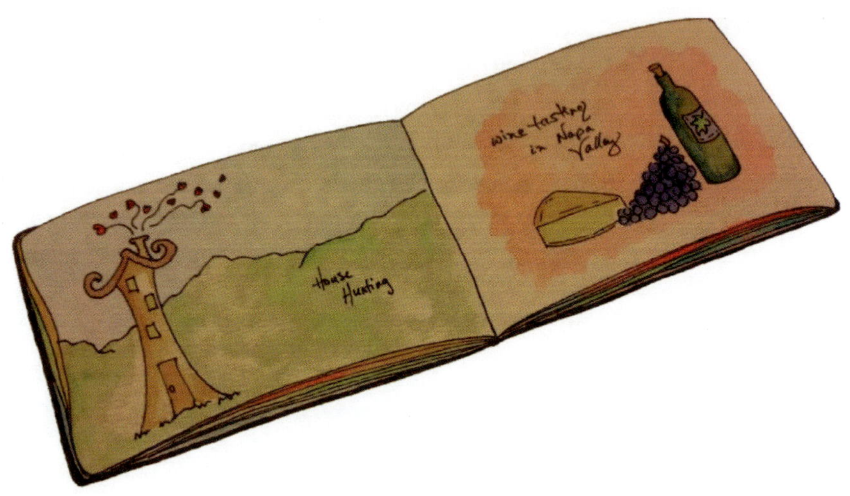

Fig.7

There are several watercolor journals on the market, but my personal favorite is the Moleskine Watercolour Album. It is firmly bound with a hard cover, easy to lay open flat, and has an attached elastic band to keep it closed and protect the pages during travel. It comes in a variety of sizes, but I prefer the 5" x 8.25" size. While compactness is important when it comes to my traveling watercolor kit, I find the smaller notebooks just aren't large enough to capture the whole scene and still have room for writing notes. Over time you may try different sizes to see which is your personal favorite, but for your first journal, I recommend using the 5" x 8.25" size. Note: Not all Moleskines are made with watercolor paper, so read the label.

THE PENCIL, ERASER AND WATERPROOF MARKER

As you will see in the next chapter, this technique of watercolor journaling requires a regular pencil, a pencil eraser, and a black waterproof marker. Most of the time I use an Ultra Fine Point Sharpie, but I also like Sakura Pigma Micron pens. The main point (*pun intended, of course*) is that it needs to be a waterproof pen so there are no smudges and smears when painting over it. Note: The special Sharpie pens that "won't bleed through paper" are *not* waterproof. (Learned that one the hard way.)

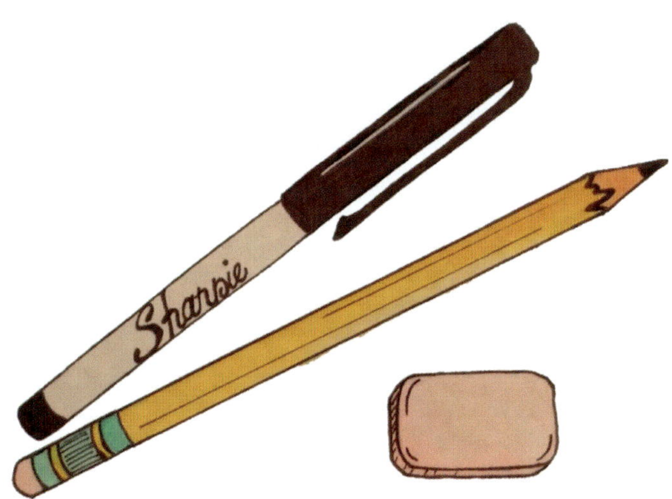

Fig.8

Keepin' It Together

I keep a set of supplies in a small tote bag that fits easily into my backpack or large purse, so it's handy whenever there's a minute or two to add to my journal. Brightly colored bags are my favorites since they are easy to find in my "creatively chaotic" house, plus they just make me smile.

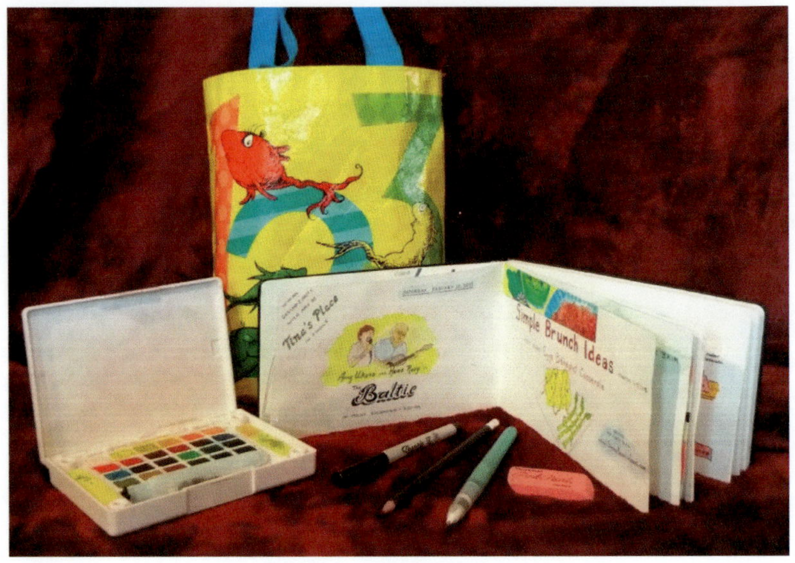

Fig.9

Bringing Down the Cost

It is easy to get carried away with buying art supplies, but a watercolor journaling kit can be put together rather inexpensively. You can get a palette of watercolors at most dollar stores, and any regular pencil and eraser will do. Water brushes are the key to making watercolor journaling quick, easy and mess-free, but you really only need one (currently cost about $4 to $8 at art stores or Amazon.com).

The one place I would encourage you not to skimp at all is on the journal itself. Moleskines are spendy ($15 to $25 currently), so try to buy when on sale or with a coupon. But keep in mind that one Moleskine journal will actually last quite a while even if you are doing two or three paintings a day.

CHAPTER 3

EASY AS 1-2-3

Before we get to the technique, I want to state emphatically that there is no right or wrong way to do art. I am not saying this is how anyone *should* draw or paint. I am simply sharing a process that I use in hopes that it might help someone else get started. It's a modification of the process my friend taught me years ago, and you may modify it a little or a lot. I'm not an authority in art or drawing or painting or much of anything really. I hope hundreds, *nay, thousands* of people will read this book, but I will consider it a great success if even one person discovers the joy of watercolor journaling from reading it. So here goes.

STEP ONE: PENCIL

Begin drawing lightly with a pencil. There's no need for precision; just draw a simple sketch of the scene or object. Regardless of your skill level, try to do this very quickly so you don't get caught up in too many details or overthink it. You do not need to draw everything in the scene or include every detail of the items you select. One object or person may be all you need to represent this experience in your journal. Remember, less can be more.

As an example, I'll use a picture of the pastry counter at my favorite bakery. First I sketch the basic shapes of the counter, the pans and the sign. I draw lightly with a pencil and erase to clean up the sketch as I go. Remember that even high quality watercolor paper erodes with too much erasing, so be gentle or wait until you have more to erase.

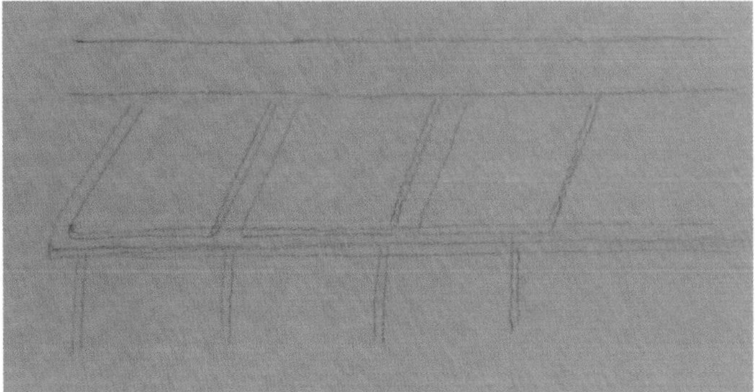
Fig.10

Then I add some details—the shapes of the baked goods, the letters on the sign.

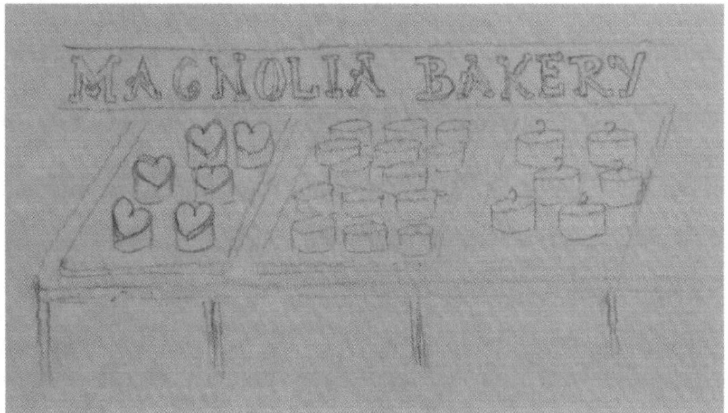

Fig.11

I keep sketching, drawing over any lines I don't like, until I'm satisfied with the basic design. Sometimes I go into great detail in my pencil sketch, and other times it's a very sketchy (*haha!*) outline. You'll note that I didn't draw the entire counter, the people, the cash register, the plates. I just sketched a few trays to represent what was most exciting to me about the visit—cupcakes, of course!

STEP TWO: SHARPIE

Once I'm satisfied with my pencil sketch, I use a Sharpie to trace only the lines that I want to keep and ignore the lines I don't like. I also add in some shading and additional detail.

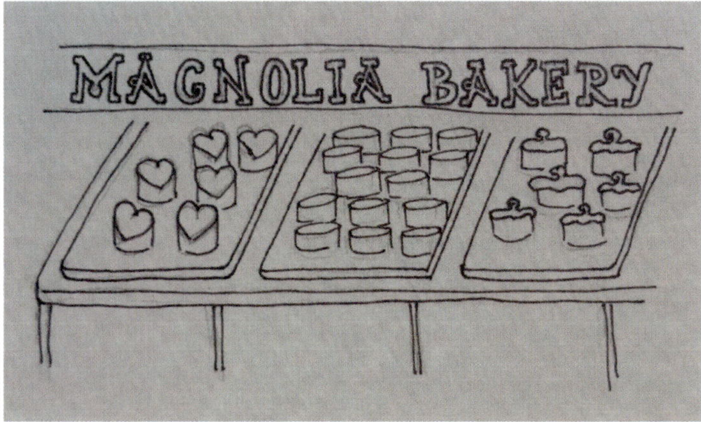

Fig.12

Then I erase all the pencil markings and the drawing is complete.

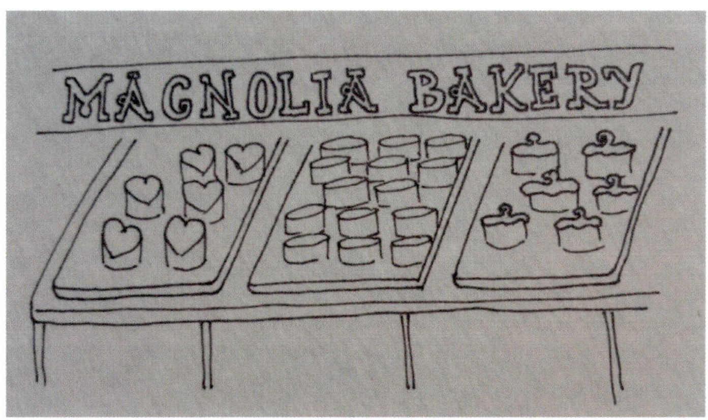

Fig.13

STEP THREE: WATERCOLOR

Finally, using my water brush, I begin adding color. Most times I just color in the various items in the picture, because I'm a color-inside-the-lines kind of gal. But depending on my mood and the journal entry, I might go wild and use a wash of color over the whole page. No rules. Play. Make your journal your own.

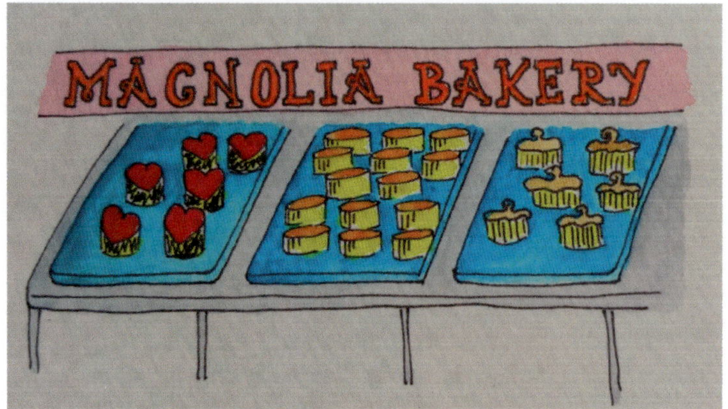

Fig.14

CAN'T COUNT TO THREE?

As simple as three steps are, the original technique my friend taught me was only two steps. She does a very quick sketch with a Sharpie and colors it in with watercolor. That's it. So try that approach to see if it works well for you. I added the pencil step because it allows me to draw the basic shapes and try out different proportions before commiting to ink. Admittedly, I have a fear of commitment, but I actually think it's helpful for beginners and people who aren't confident in their drawing skills to start with the pencil step.

CHAPTER 4

BECOME A SHAPE SHIFTER

Remember laying on the grass in the park, taking turns with a friend pointing out pictures in the clouds? Oh look! That cloud looks like a clown with a little head and great big shoes. There's a banana split with a cherry on top. Yum!

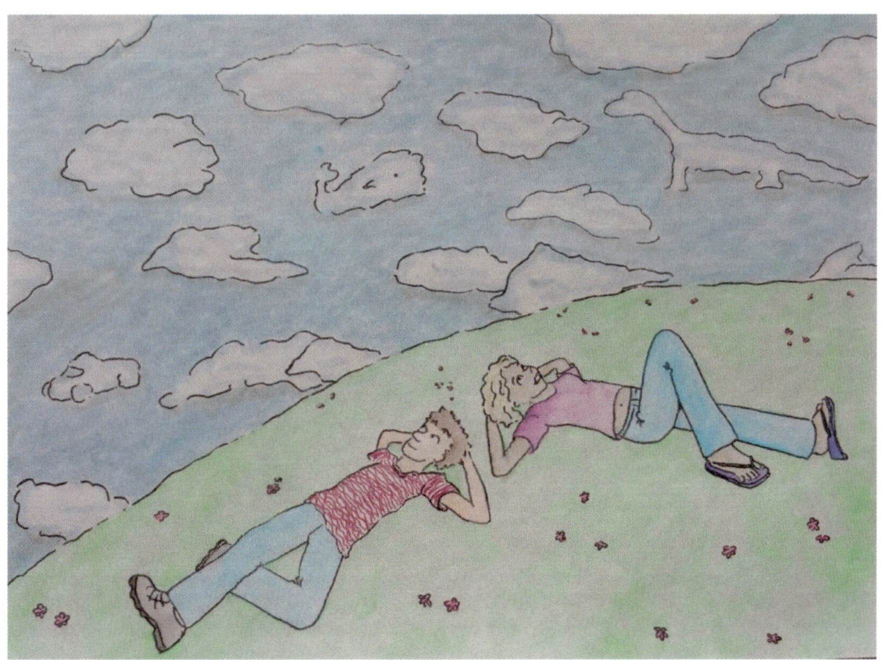

Fig.15

With just a little imagination you can begin to see shapes in everything around you. A skyscraper is a tall rectangle with hundreds of small rectangle windows in rows. A sailboat is a triangle sail beside a straight pole on top of a half circle. The letter S can be a snake. The letter T, a telephone pole.

Before you begin a sketch, sit for a moment and really look at what you are about to draw. Look for basic shapes: circles, squares, triangles, rectangles, diamonds, cubes, ellipses. Sketch the shapes you see and place them on the page in relation to the other shapes. Once you like the placement and shapes, then sketch in the details, softening the edges of the shapes and morphing them into one another as needed.

For example, here's a picture of an apartment building. First locate the shapes—the square and rectangle windows, the rectangle air conditioners, the half circles above the windows, the Z-shaped fire escape. Then draw the shapes on the page and add the details to complete the picture.

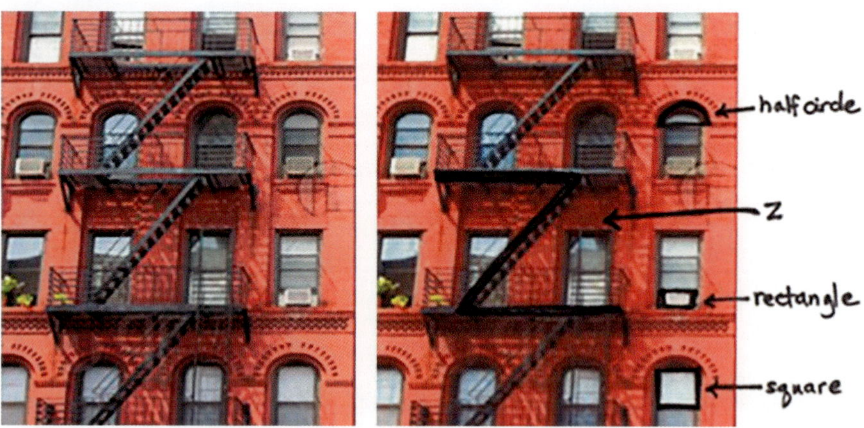

Fig.16

An easy way to practice seeing shapes in pictures is to take the weekly grocery store advertisements and highlight the shapes you see in the adds.

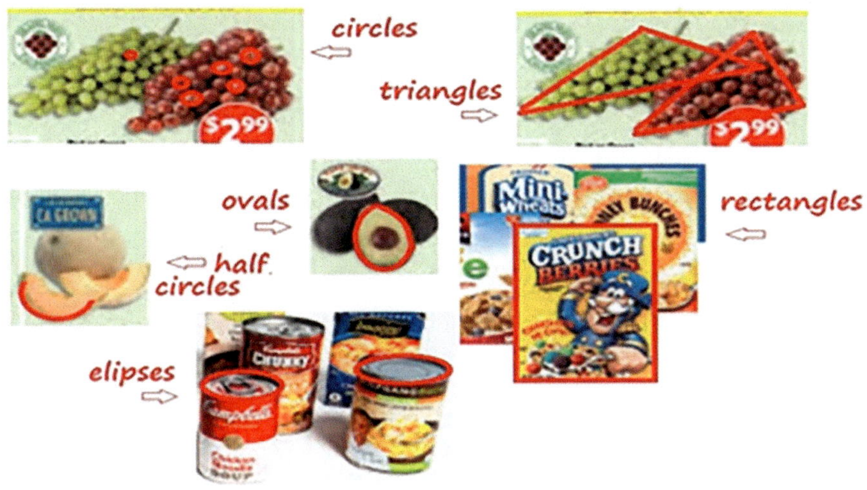

Fig.17

This practice will help develop your artistic eye for seeing the basic shapes that form the structure for everything and create muscle memory for drawing these shapes accurately.

Perhaps this is a good time to address the issue of whether copying and tracing are "cheating." When a child in school is given a handout from the teacher to trace the letter A a dozen times and then to copy it many more, it's not cheating, it's learning how to write the letter A. When we are learning to draw something, it is helpful to trace or copy it several times to develop muscle memory and hand-eye coordination. Then in the future when we want to draw that object or something similar, we will know how to do it. I will quite often do a Google search for an image I don't know how to draw, such as a person jogging. I search through the images available until I find one similar to the position I have in mind. I print it out and either trace or copy it, modifying it to create the picture I want to draw. Now if you get **too** good at this, it's called forgery and is a felony, but I don't think most of us need to worry about that happening. I also enjoy YouTube tutorials that show step-by-step how to draw or paint something. In fact, the painting on the cover of this book was done by following a YouTube tutorial by Jennifer Branch—I love her watercolors! When I create a painting while someone walks me through the steps, it's still my painting even though credit for the design and instruction lies with someone else, in this case Jennifer Branch (and she graciously granted permission for me to use this painting in publication). So copy and trace as much as you like as you learn to see and draw shapes.

A sewing teacher once told me the secret to making even the most elaborate dress was simply to sew one seam at a time, followed by the next and the next. That advice works for sketching, too—just draw one shape at a time, followed by the next and the next.

Chapter 5

VOLUME CONTROL

Whenever we try something new, especially artistic or creative, most of us experience a barrage of thoughts telling us that we are deficient, not good enough, less than others, or somehow inadequate. This is commonly referred to as the inner critic, and it can interfere with our ability to try new things and stretch ourselves.

Through the years I have allowed those thoughts to shame and silence me far too many times, and on the occasions that I was brave enough to perform in public or show my art to people anyway, the inner critic turned up the volume so high I often felt like saying to people around me, *"I'm sorry, is the noise in my head bothering you?"*

If your critic is anything like mine, it expects you to be an expert at something the first time you try. When I missed the first free throw I ever tried, it said, *"See, you can't even make a basket. You'll never make the team, so give it up."* But I didn't give up, I kept practicing and eventually did make the team. Of course, then the critic upped the ante and said, *"You'll never make varsity, so give it up."* But I kept practicing and not only made the varsity team, but then college and later, the pros. No wait, that was someone else. I gave up after one season and proved it right. Shucks.

I no longer am willing to let the inner critic rob me of the joy of trying new things, especially creative pursuits such as watercolor journaling. Below are ten strategies to use when dealing with the inner critic.

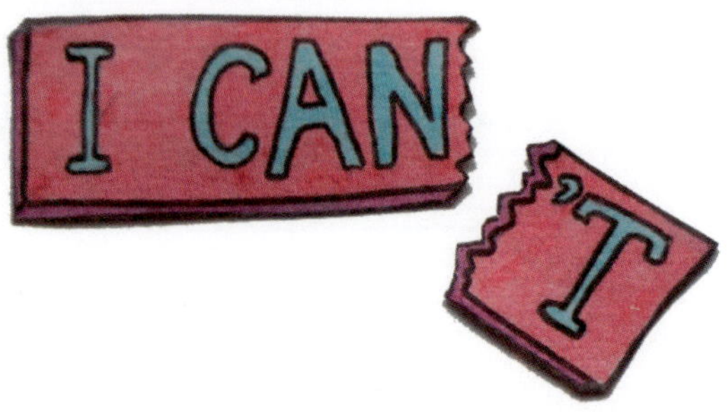

Fig.18

UNDERSTAND AND APPRECIATE THE CRITIC

We forget sometimes that we are mammals, creatures of instinct, and that these instincts are essential to our survival as a species. One instinct is to maintain homeostasis—the status quo. It is safer to keep things stable and predictable. We need this survival mechanism when dealing with life-and-death issues. If you're tempted to race in front of an oncoming train because you're running late, your brain sends a message that you're not capable of doing that and shouldn't even try. Listen to that voice—please!

The problem comes when that instinct tries with the same intensity to protect us from disappointment or humiliation. It replays our past failings and embarrass-ments, all the way back to when we wet our pants (and the floor) during the first grade talent show (yes, that was me), and warns us it's going to be even worse this time.

The thing is, it is almost always relying on old information or on things our parents or teachers said when we were young. It doesn't take into account the fact that we've grown, learned, changed and, maybe, just maybe, our parents were wrong in the first place. Besides, disappointment and humiliation don't kill. They don't even maim. And few really good things happen without dreaming big, taking risks and trying new things.

So appreciate the voice that shouts *"Give it up!"* or *"Don't show your painting to anyone!"* but don't follow its advice. It has your best interests at heart—it's just wrong. Reassure the critic that you are not taking a serious risk here—you're not quitting your day job to become a full time watercolor journalist. It's just a hobby—just a new skill you are learning for fun.

EDUCATE THE CRITIC

Chances are your inner critic isn't a particularly reliable judge of what's cool and has a very narrow definition of art. Spend some time at a museum of modern art and see the vast array of things that are considered to be art. I personally have a lot of trouble keeping smart aleck remarks to myself when I see certain exhibits that look as if a toddler created them or, worse, like nothing was created at all (such as a blank canvas entitled "Nothingness of Being"). But this helps me to understand that art is truly in the eye of the beholder and to appreciate anything I create simply because I created it. The images and colors produce something unique that didn't exist before. They came from within me and were produced by me, and I can take joy in that.

Imagine for a moment that you painted a picture of your beloved Aunt Nellie and it turned out like this:

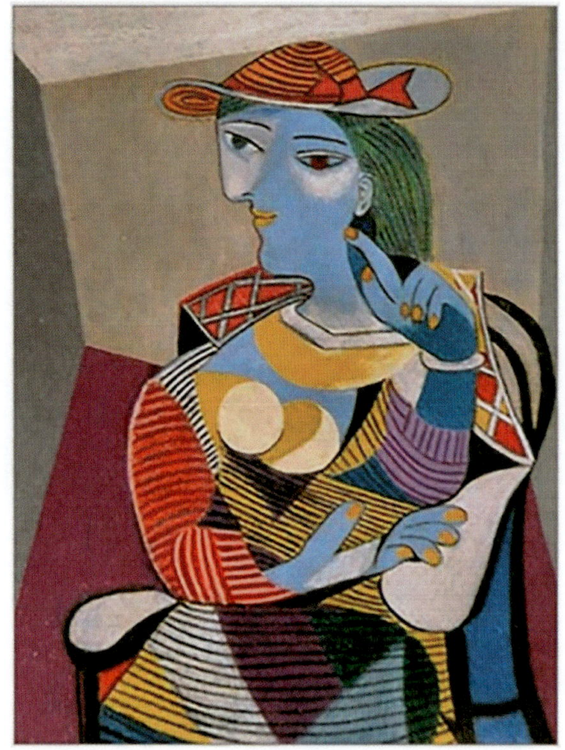

Fig.19

Your inner critic would have a field day with it, laughing at the fact that both eyes are on the same side of the face and warning you to never let others see this, especially Aunt Nellie, *God forbid!* Yet this is a Picasso painting worth millions of dollars. Now Picasso was a brilliant and talented artist, and his paintings didn't "turn out" this way because he lacked skill. He chose to use colors and images and distortions of reality to create some pretty interesting and unique art. So let your distortions, whether purposeful or accidental, be a valid part of the art process.

"I paint objects as I think them,
not as I see them."
—Pablo Picasso

26

An impressionistic painter who was teaching a class at Yosemite National Park a few years ago explained to me that he might see a tree in one place, a mountain in another, and a rippling brook in yet another, and then combine them into one painting to become his *impression* of Yosemite. He might paint a splotch of blue with a dab of beige on top of it, and it would become his *impression* of a person. Leave "reality" to the camera and just add your *impression* of the moment to your journal.

REMIND THE CRITIC OF YOUR SUCCESSES

Do you remember a time in your life when you couldn't tie your shoes? It seemed impossibly complex with a series of tasks that required fine motor skills you simply didn't possess. Yet today you tie your shoes in seconds without even looking at your fingers and while carrying on an animated conversation.

Take a moment to list all the things you once found impossible but now do with ease. I'll start the list for you: 1) sitting up; 2) rolling over; 3) feeding yourself; 4) crawling; 5) walking; 6) talking; 8) dressing yourself; 9) saying your ABCs; 10) reading.... Keep going. There are literally thousands of skills you have now that you did not have at birth, and any number of those are more difficult than watercolor journaling. You are amazing! You have learned so much in your life already, and this is just one more thing. And before you start in with the old-dog-new-tricks excuse, forget it. It's simply not true. Not for dogs and certainly not for humans. People well into their 90s have learned to play a new instrument or speak a new language. So remind your inner critic (aka yourself) of your life-long habit of success at learning new things and pick up that paintbrush.

AGREE WITH THE CRITIC AND LAUGH

I've gotten pretty good at doodling and simple drawing over the years, but I still have a dickens of a time drawing faces. Time and time again, I've drawn a picture of a very attractive person only to make him look hideous because I can't draw his face. And expressions? Forget it. Sometimes I'm trying to make someone look happy and they end up looking absolutely maniacal. And I'll admit that I don't usually show Aunt Nellie the Picasso-esque distortion I've drawn for fear she'll think that's how I see her. But I have learned to just laugh and say, "*OMG! I have GOT to learn to draw faces one of these days!!*" I will continue to practice drawing faces and maybe take classes or watch YouTube tutorials to improve my skills. But in the meantime, laughter is good medicine.

THANK THE CRITIC

When I am daydreaming, "*Wouldn't it be great if I won Dancing With the Stars?*" my inner critic usually says, with a hint of sarcasm, "*Oh sure, honey, dream on.*" There's no threat of upsetting the status quo by mere wishing. But when I seriously entertain the idea of trying something new or taking steps to make it happen, the inner critic takes notice and says, "*Hey, wait, Wait, WAIT!*" Then it begins the barrage of reasons that it's impossible and increases the warnings to turn back now. Begin to recognize the increased noise and messages of fear as an indication of just how important this new thing is to you. I have finally learned to say to the critic, *"Thank you for showing me how much I really want this by how loud you are being."* Gratitude can be a very powerful tool.

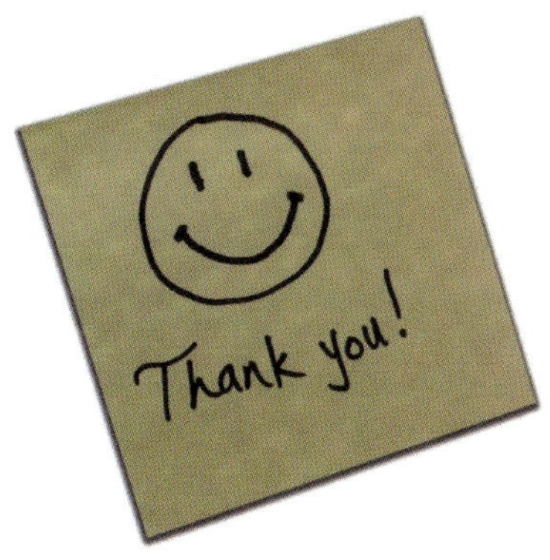

Fig.20

SMILE ALL THE WHILE

We have always known that happiness can produce a smile, but did you know a smile can produce happiness? Recent studies have indicated that 15 minutes a day of smiling (even a forced smile) may actually be as effective in treating depression in some patients as antidepressants. Try this: smile really big for 30 seconds and see how you feel. Go ahead. I'll wait. It doesn't solve life's problems, but it does give an instant lift to your energy. How does that apply here? Smile while you draw or paint. Remember to enjoy the moment, the creative process. Be happy in the doing without concern for the results.

KEEP YOUR EYES ON YOUR OWN WORK

I remember my teachers telling me that a lot in grade school, and it's still good advice: Keep your eyes on your own work. Comparisons to others can be an effective tool for the inner critic, either convincing us that we are inadequate or overinflating our egos to undermine our efforts. But there is no need to compare your work to anyone else's. There will always be someone better and someone worse at anything we try, so what does it really matter? Just enjoy your own creation simply because it's yours.

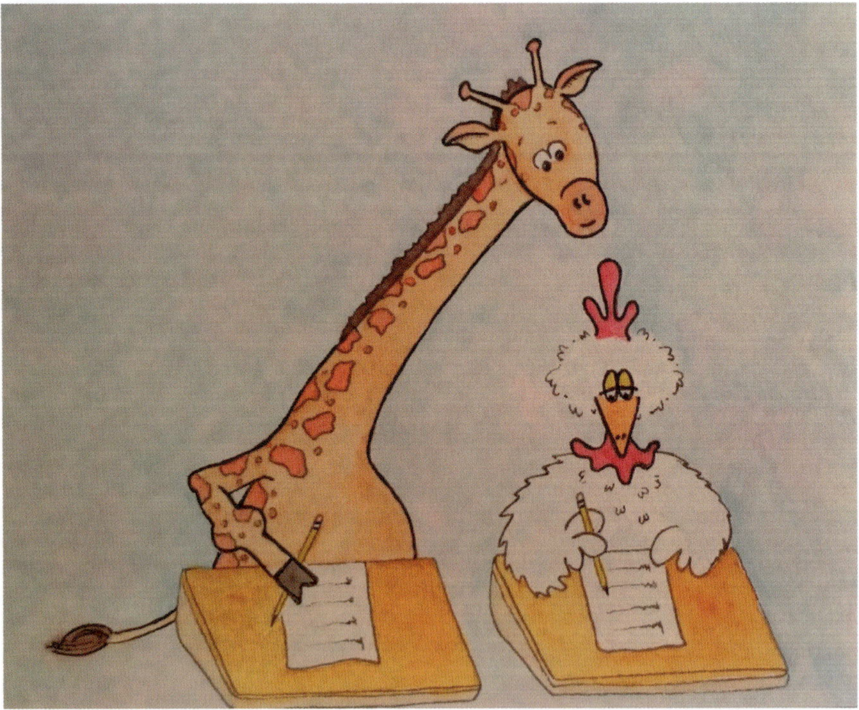

Fig.21

ASSIGN THE CRITIC A JOB

The inner critic is very serious about your security and survival, so assign it the task of protecting you from living too small—make that Enemy #1. What a waste to go through life never taking chances or trying new things! Ask the critic to nudge you whenever you are playing it too safe and to encourage you to try new things.

IGNORE THE CRITIC

What? How can I just ignore the critic? By remembering that the thoughts you are having are just thoughts. They are automatically generated by the brain in response to certain stimuli. They don't mean anything. You don't have to act on them. You don't have to engage or argue with them. You don't have to figure out the deep psychological reasons for them. You don't have to blame anyone for them. Simply accept they are just thoughts, and thoughts come and go. It's your mind, and you can choose which thoughts to entertain and which ones to ignore. Like most things, it just takes a bit of practice.

ACT AS IF

Use your imagination combined with a physical action. Reach out your arm and pretend to turn down the volume control on a stereo as you visualize the inner critic's comments fading to a low din. Put your finger to your lips and say "Shhh!" as if you're a librarian shushing the inner critic. Physically acting out a mental picture can sometimes be very powerful in changing an emotional state.

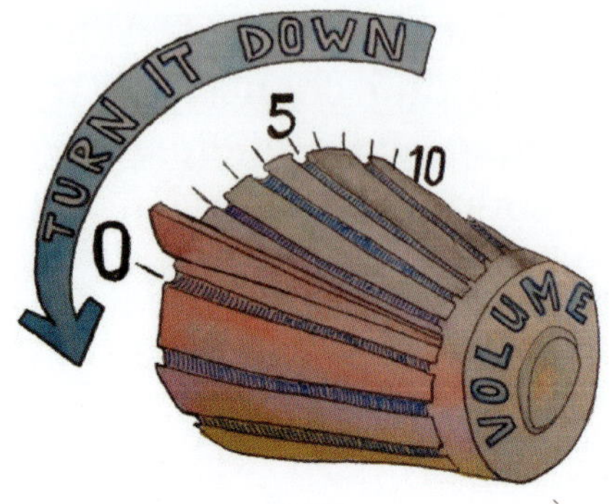

Fig.22

Not all of these techniques will work for everyone or for every occasion, of course. But I hope you'll find one or two especially helpful.

CHAPTER 6

LOOKIT, LOOKIT WHAT I DID!

No one wants to sit through a slideshow of your latest trip *(do kids today even know what a slideshow is?)*, but they will happily look at your watercolor journal, complimenting you with the turn of each page. *"You painted this?"* they'll exclaim in amazement. Even when your drawings don't turn out the way you wanted, friends will see them and say, *"I wish I could draw like that,"* and they'll laugh when you tell them that they could. Go ahead, soak up the acclaim and keep them in the dark if you want to about how easy it really is.

I'll share with you now a watercolor journal I did when I visited New York shortly after my friend introduced me to this technique. The fact that some of my drawings are, well, less than fabulous, let's say, just shows that simple drawings and colors can add personality and fun to a travel record regardless of the artistic quality. Plus, the more you do it, the better you'll get, and that can be really fun to see your drawings improve over time. I can't tell you how many times I have surprised myself and wanted to squeal like a child in amazement, *"Lookit what I did!"*

The NOTEs below the pictures comment on techniques used for adding variety and visual interest or discuss "mistakes" that illustrate the point that skill and perfection are not necessary in order to enjoy watercolor journaling.

If you see a picture and your inner critic starts up with thoughts that you could never draw that, pause a moment and look for the shapes in the picture as discussed in Chapter 4. And remember, you get to erase it and try again and again.

I used a 5" x 8.25" Moleskine Watercolour Album. On the front cover I glued a photograph taken from the top of the Brooklyn Bridge.

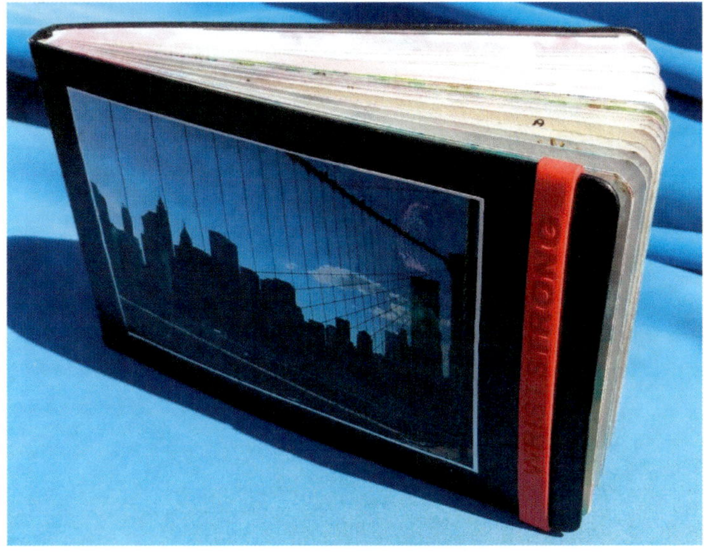
Fig.23

On the inside cover I painted my destination and flight arrangements.

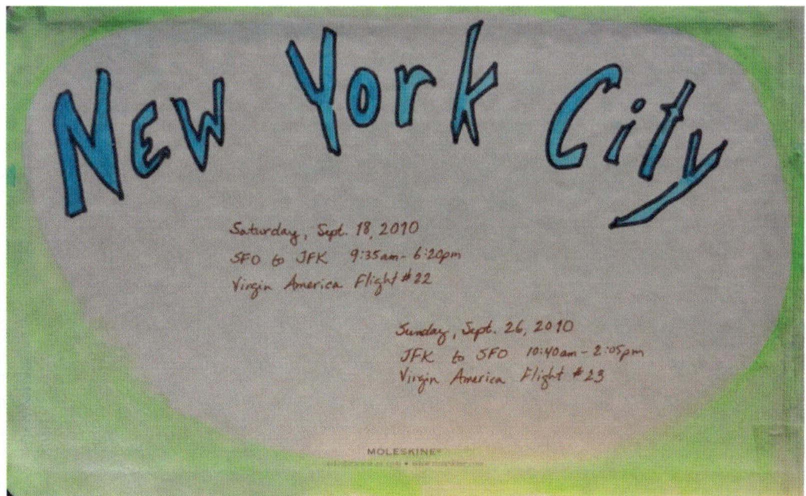

Fig.24

The day before I left for New York, my friends stood around my cubicle at work and rapid-fired all the places I just *had* to see in New York, naming them faster than I could write them down. I did manage to squeeze most of their recommendations into my trip, though, and am so glad I did.

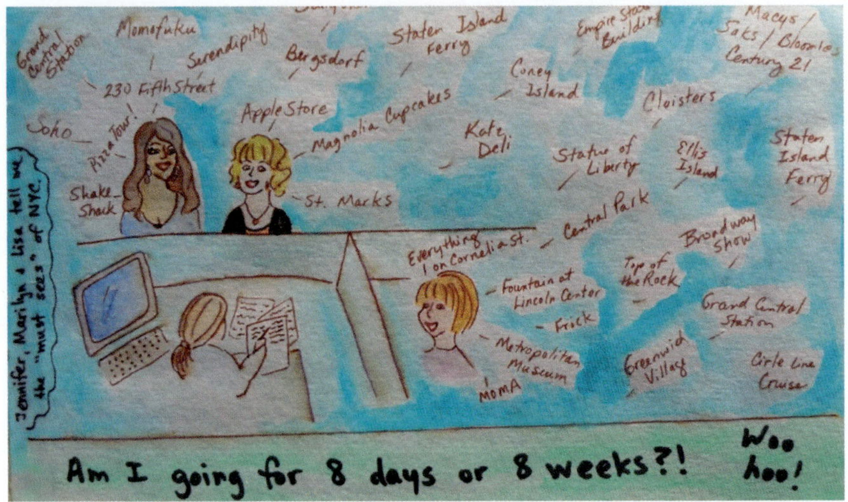

Fig.25

NOTE: Remember what I shared earlier about the challenge of drawing faces? Well, believe you me, this picture looks nothing like my beautiful friends, but it still reminds me of that animated conversation and how excited they were for me to be seeing the Big Apple for the first time.

New York City is such an iconic place, and my very first experience upon arriving was a stereotypical taxi ride. Great Scott! In order to subdue fears for my life, I pretended I was on a rollercoaster as we darted from one lane to the next, being jolted side-to-side, holding my breath. Whew! No need for coffee after a few near-death experiences on the ride from the airport to my friend's apartment.

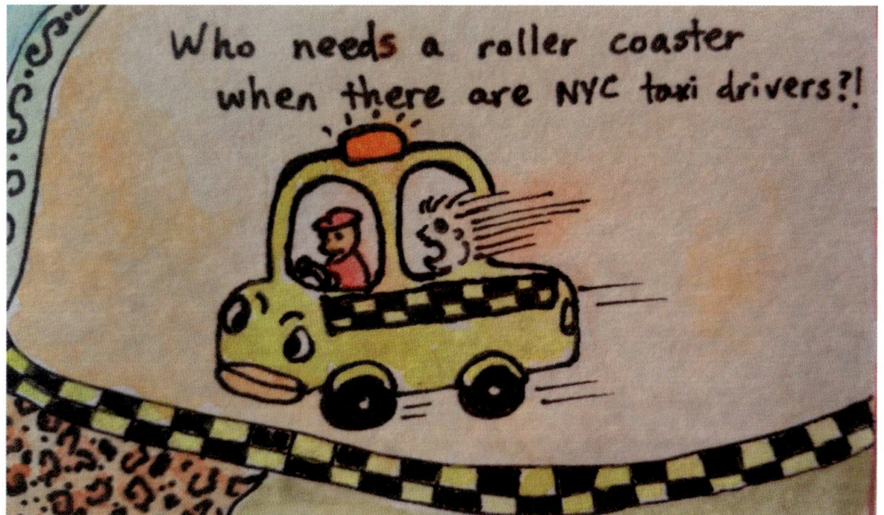

Fig.26

NOTE: It's fun to personify an object in a painting, such as drawing the headlights and front bumper of this taxi to look like a face to give the appearance that the taxi is alive and actually the one responsible for my harrowing ride.

The first day of my trip included a flight from San Francisco to JFK Airport, the great taxi adventure, and meeting my friend Tracey's three cats, Jessie, Gotham and Nikkie, who provided great entertainment throughout my weeklong visit.

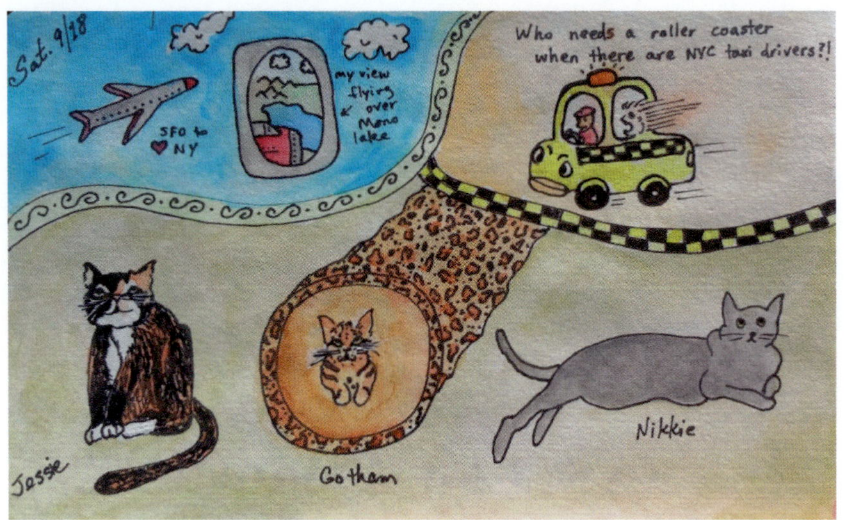

Fig.27

NOTE: One way to add visual interest to a journal is to vary the number of items per page. On this one, I combined all three sketches from the day on one page, using borders to separate them.

Tracey spoiled me from the first *(I like that in a person!)* by providing a breakfast of crumpets and ginger spread. Yum! At the time of this vacation, I was on a major exercise kick and wanted to find a gym I could use for the week. To my pleasant surprise, Planet Fitness was running a special to join for only $5 for the first month, cancel at any time, and even gave me a free tee shirt! So cool! I had fun painting their logo. Then Tracey and I took the A train, a la Ella Fitzgerald, as we began our tour of the Big Apple. The velvety voice of Ella sang in my head throughout the week... *Take the A Train... Drop Me Off in Harlem... Autumn in New York....*

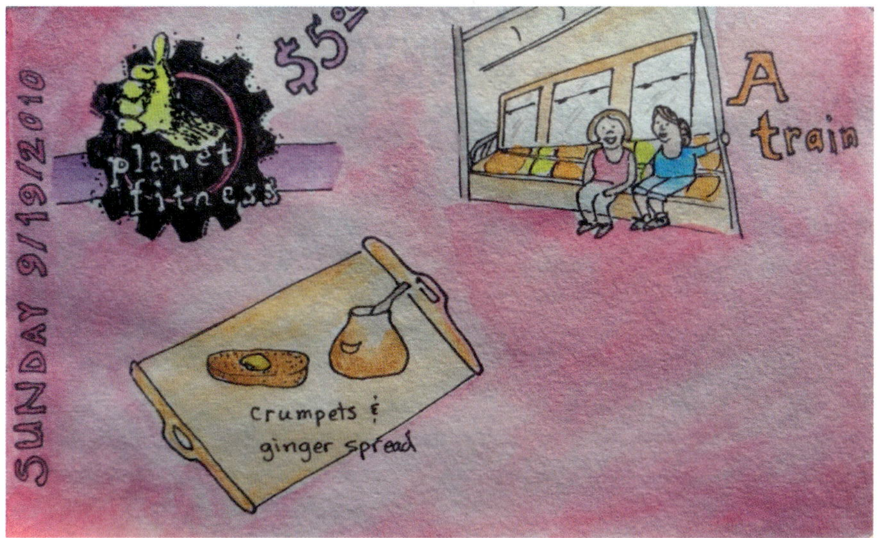

Fig.28

NOTE: I use artistic license almost as often as my driver's license. The crumpets and ginger spread weren't served on a tray—we sat together at the breakfast table. But this simplified the sketch for my journal. Also, while neither my friend Tracey nor I would be mistaken for supermodels, we look far better than this drawing on the A Train. Again, it just makes me laugh when I see it. (Tracey, hope you're laughing, too!)

Our first sightseeing stop was Coney Island, riding on the Cyclone (my favorite rollercoaster ride ever!) the Wonder Wheel, and eating lunch at Nathan's.

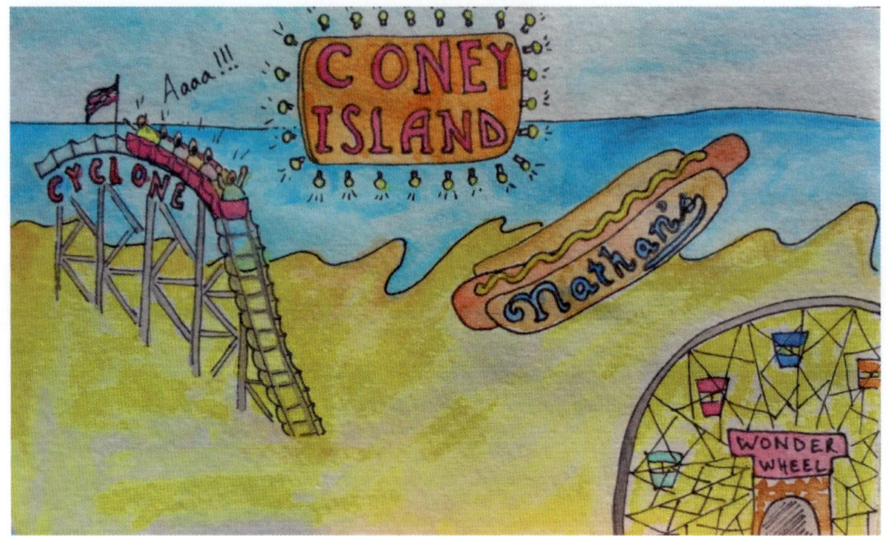

Fig.29

NOTE: I imagine that an actual watercolor artist's painting of Coney Island wouldn't include a hot dog laying in the sand that's as big as the giant rollercoaster beside it. But for watercolor journaling, you can create a collage of pictures and logos that don't need to be drawn to scale but that represent the day or experience.

Continuing the iconic tour of NYC, we walked through Greenwich Village, in awe of its amazing musical and cultural history.

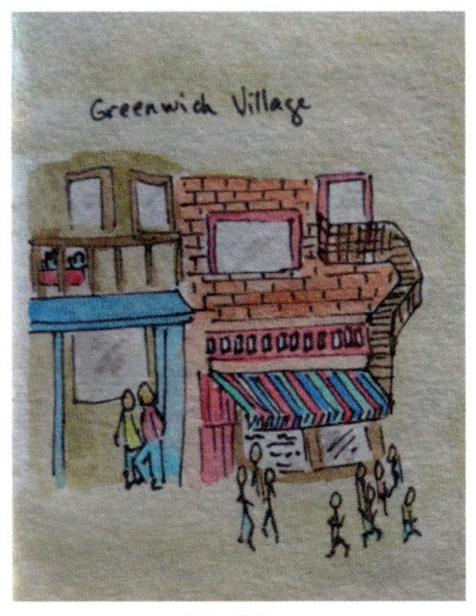

Fig.30

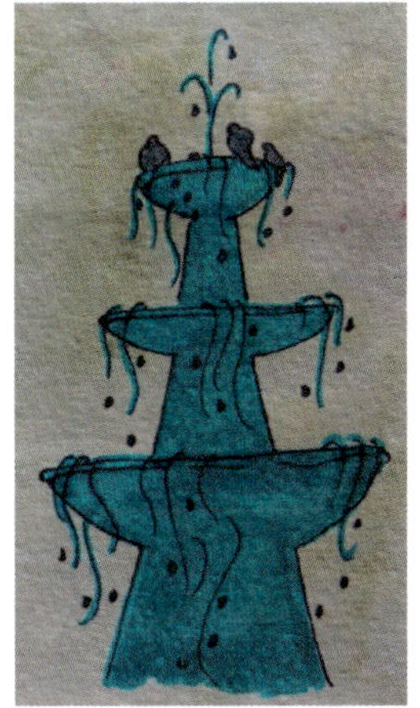

Fig.31

NOTE: Be an impressionistic painter— stick figures are perfectly fine *impressions* of people in watercolor journaling.

On Monday, Tracey went to work, and I began my solo exploration with a three-hour cruise on the Circle-Line. The tour guide was particularly entertaining and informative, and the sights were beautiful. The boat ride was relaxing and gave me plenty of time to sketch and paint while enjoying the lapping water, the cool breeze and the sights of New York.

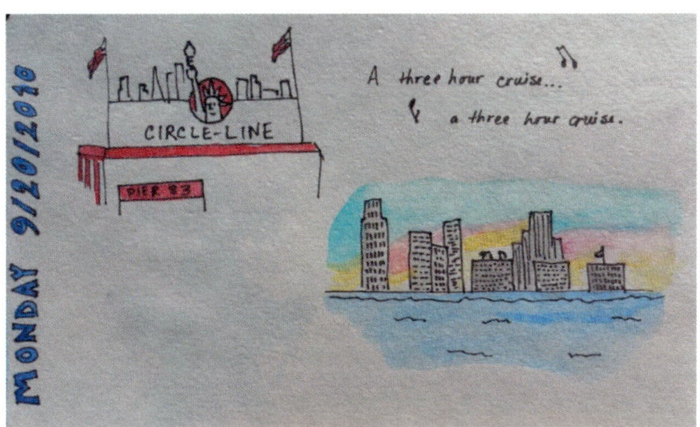

Fig.32

NOTE: No need to stress when you don't have time to sketch and paint each day. It should add to your enjoyment of the day, not add to your To Do list. You can either just skip a day, or you can make pencil notes reserving the pages in your journal for what you want to sketch and take care to capture photos with your camera of the angles you'll want to review. I had spent Sunday sightseeing and talking with Tracey and didn't want to sketch during our limited time together. Since I had taken photos and made notes, I was able to use time on the boat tour Monday to sketch my pictures from Sunday.

After the boat tour I walked across the Brooklyn Bridge. This is by far the number one *Must-See* recommendation that I give everyone traveling to New York. It is a very easy walk and such an incredible view of the iconic bridge and a panoramic view of the City.

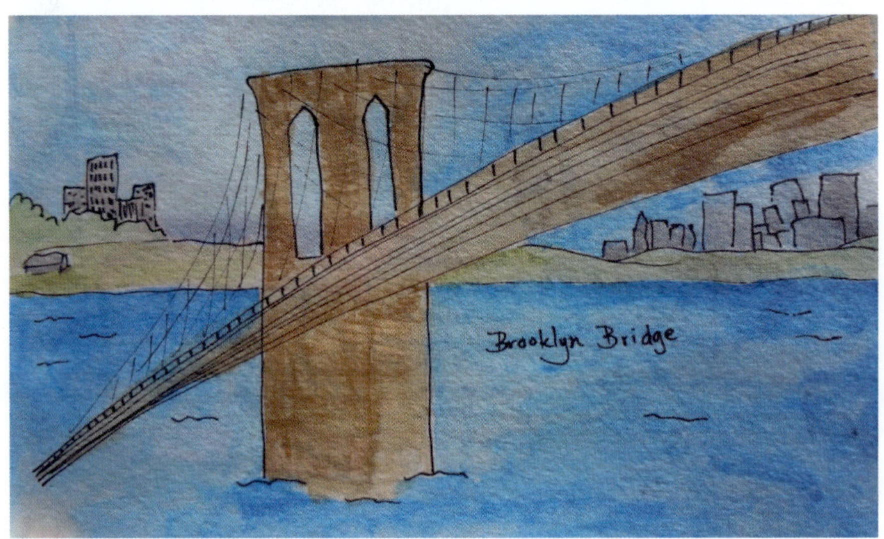

Fig.33

 According to my drawing, the Brooklyn Bridge ends in the middle of the East River which, I assure you, it does not. Journal drawings do not need to be technically accurate—no one's going to build a bridge based on my picture. And the fact is that most people won't even notice mistakes like this unless we point them out.

The next day began with a morning of shopping followed by a relaxing lunch at a sidewalk café, Arriba Arriba. I highly recommend this West Side Mexican restaurant.

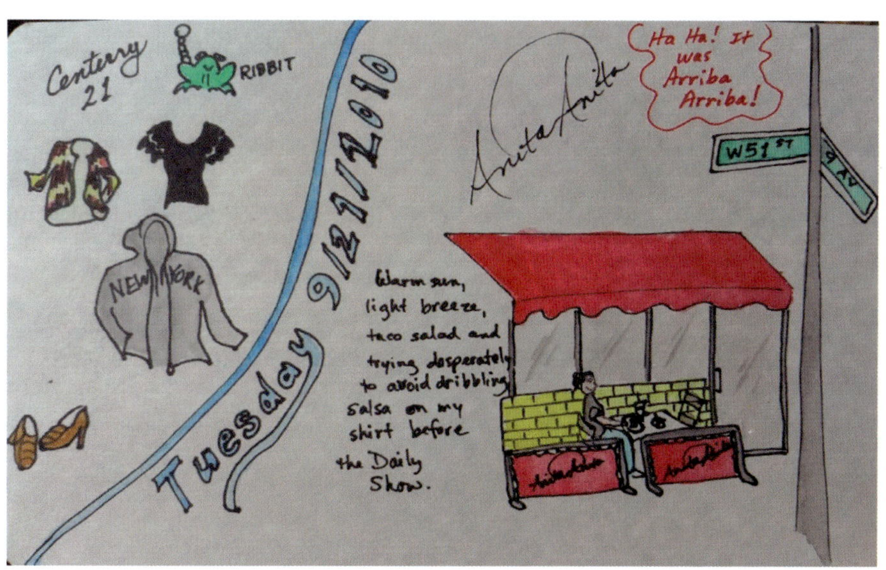

Fig.34

NOTE: I enjoy trying to copy logos and copied this one from the menu only later to discover that it was not Anita Anita. I just made a little note beside it so that I would remember the correct name. Now, a mistake like this can drive me bonkers, but it's just another opportunity to practice acceptance.

I'm a huge fan of The Daily Show with Jon Stewart and was thrilled to get a ticket to be in the studio audience for the taping of his show when Sigourney Weaver was the guest.

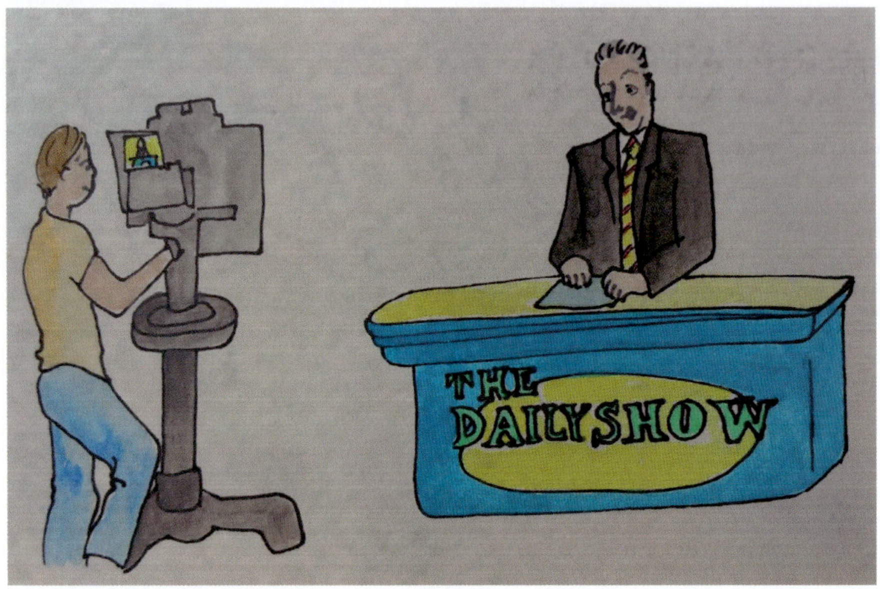

Fig.35

NOTE: While I was happy that I managed to get a sarcastic look on his face, I was still frustrated that it doesn't look like Jon Stewart. But the logo on the desk and the camera man give good clues as to who it is. The only similarity of the cameraman in my drawing to the one in real life is that he was wearing blue jeans, but again, who cares? This picture makes me happy because it reminds me how much fun I had being there.

After The Daily Show, I headed to Times Square and heard glorious gospel music which pulled me into the Times Square Church. Wow! It is a huge church with a huge choir and a huge sound. Very apropos to being on Times Square.

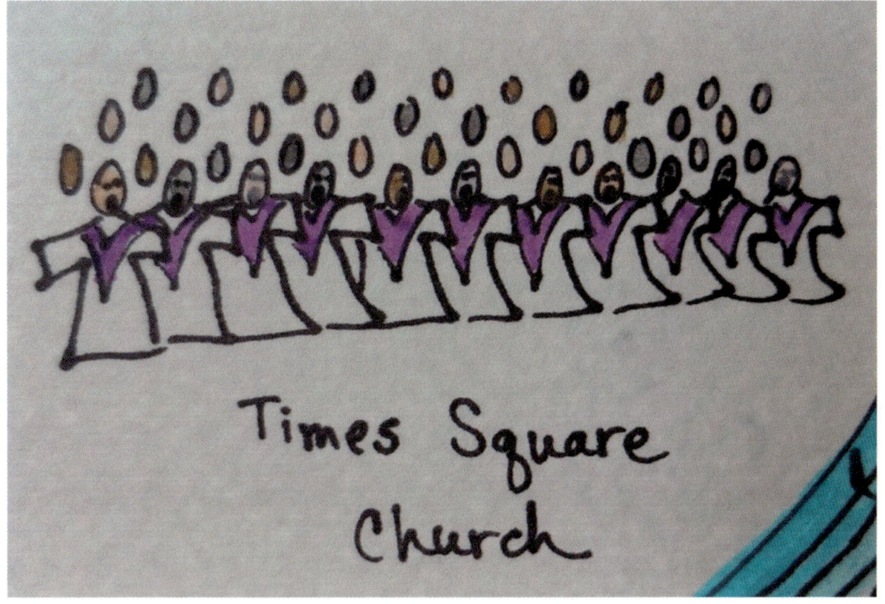

Fig.36

NOTE: This drawing is an example of when less is more. No need to draw every face or body. I didn't even draw the hands or hair of the front row singers. What was significant was their choir robes and joyous music.

One of my favorite moments in New York was meeting a street musician who introduced himself as Cesar from Santo Domingo. He not only played the violin beautifully, but he handed it to me and taught me how to play two notes. Then as I played them in the simple rhythm he taught me, he danced and said, *"Look at me! Your music is making me dance."* What fun!

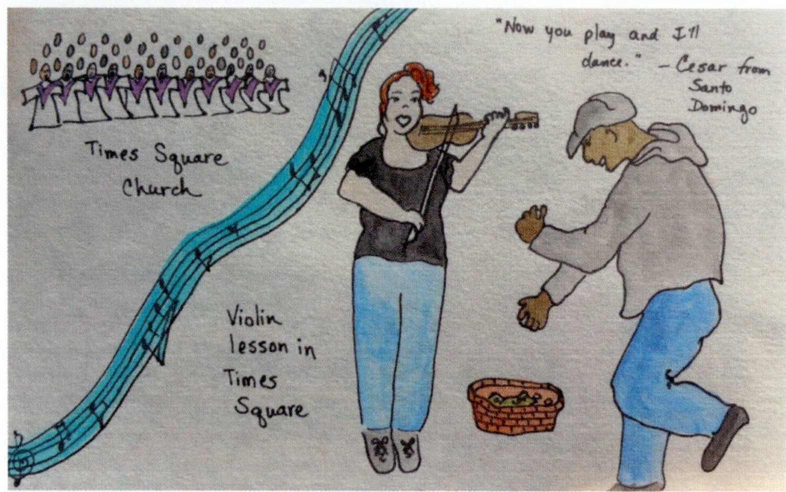

Fig.37

Yummy, yummy pizza at Famous Famiglia Pizzaria.

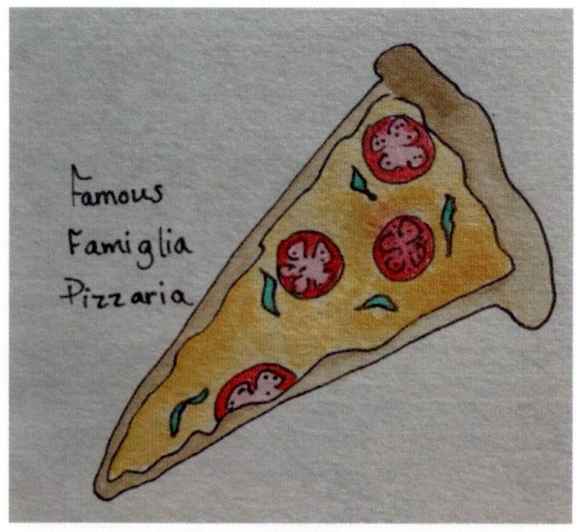

Fig.38

Such fun to walk along Broadway and see all the marquees with flashing lights. ♫ *"They say the neon lights are bright o-on Broad-way (on Broad-waaaaay)."* ♫

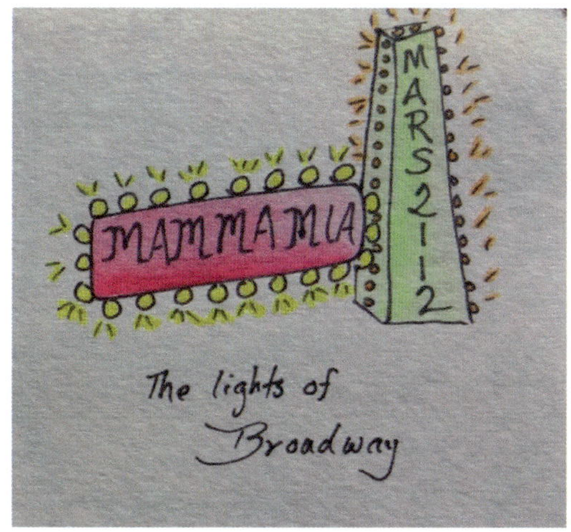

Fig.39

Ooo la lah! Breakfast at Le Pain Quotidien was lovely and delish.

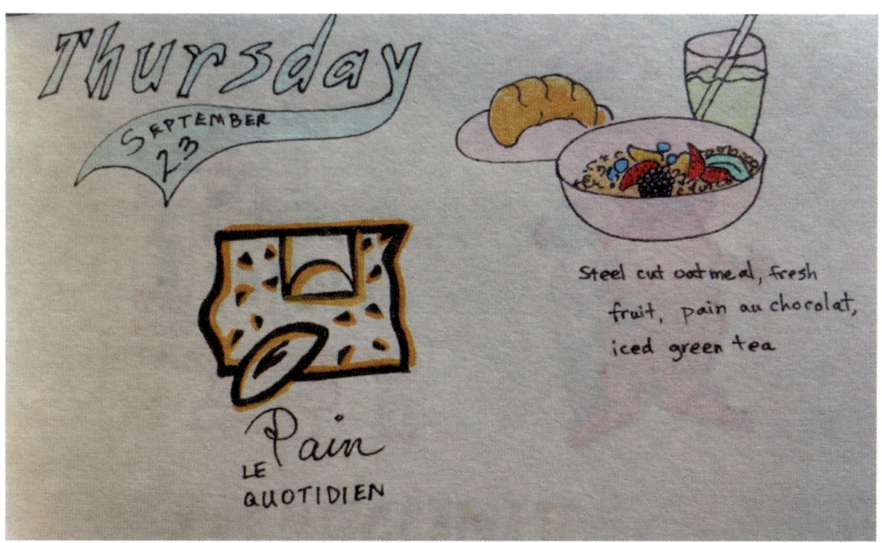

Fig.40

Tracey's cats got along pretty well while she was home, but when she was out, serious skirmishes could occur. So before leaving for work in the morning, Tracey put Nikkie in protective custody in the bedroom and left Jessie and Gotham to roam the rest of the apartment. I got up sometime later and, without thinking, walked into the bedroom to use Tracey's full-length mirror. Nikkie made her great escape, and it took nearly twenty minutes of Keystone Cops antics to get everyone back into their designated rooms. I settled for using the bathroom mirror after that.

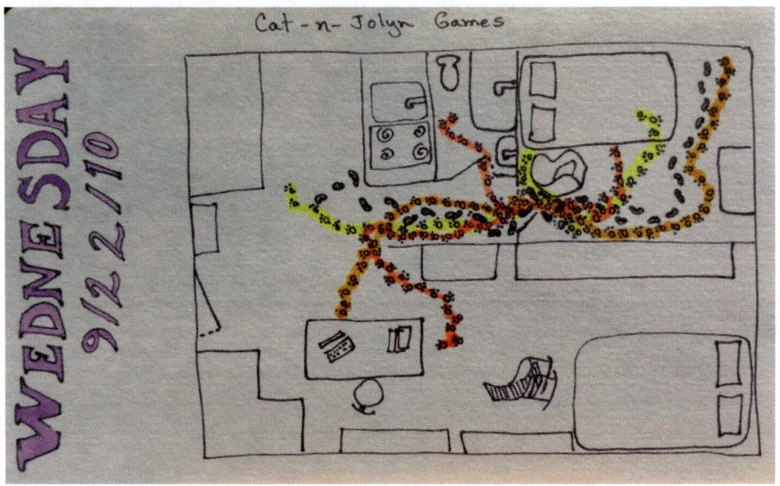

Fig.41

NOTE: One technique to create interest is to leave most of the drawing in black and white and only add color to the significant features.

A close second to the walk across the Brooklyn Bridge on my list of *Must-Sees* when visiting New York is to go on one of Scott's Pizza Tours, aptly named *"New York's Cheesiest Guided Tour."* Scott is friendly and funny and incredibly knowledgeable about pizza—it's history, where to find the best pizza and how to judge it. I'd swear he knew everyone we passed on the three-hour walking tour, and he introduced us to several shop owners. Scott taught us the "slide test" to tell whether pizza was made with freshly made (same day) mozzarella. And the best part of the tour, of course, was eating a slice of pizza at each of the three best pizzerias in New York City: Joe's, John's and Lombardi's. Mmm-MMM!

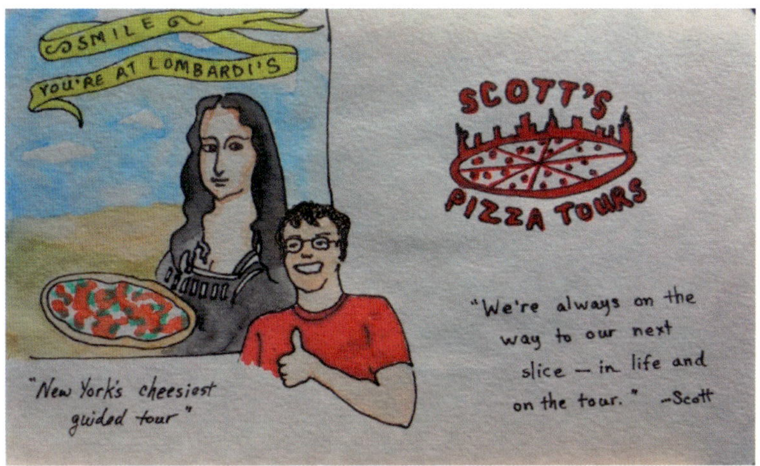

Fig.42

NOTE: Bravely share your art. The response may amaze you. I emailed Scott when I got home, thanking him for a fun tour and attaching a copy of my journal page, even though it didn't look much like him. He posted it on his website saying:

> *"Check out this stunning artwork by SPT alum Jolyn Parker. My jaw hit the floor when I opened the email containing this image. WOW!" (http://blog.scottspizzatours.com/post/16971945 95/spt-watercolor)*

How cool is that!? So share your sketches, especially the ones that make you smile.

Along the tour, we stopped at a lovely cheese market called Alleva which had been founded by Pina Alleva when she emigrated here from Benevento, Italy in 1892. Her great grandson Bob showed us how fresh mozzarella is made and gave us free samples, too. Yum!

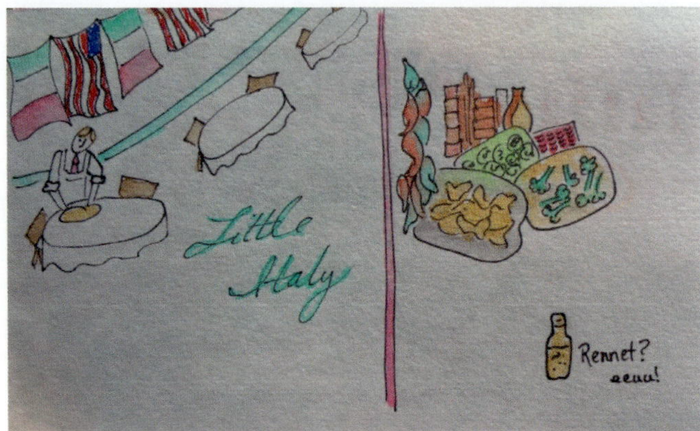

Fig.43

One very hot New York afternoon, I enjoyed a banana split while sketching until there was a melty, gooey mess in the bottom of the dish. Don't worry, I ate that, too. Oo-hoo-hoo yeah!

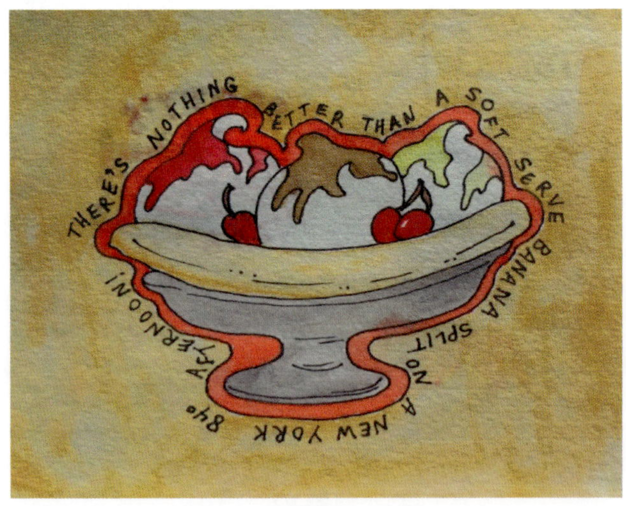

Fig.44

50

 Play with the location of your text—above, below, beside, all around your drawing. And feel free to use lots more text that I do. It's your journal—your style.

Times Square—so much to see. Don't miss it!

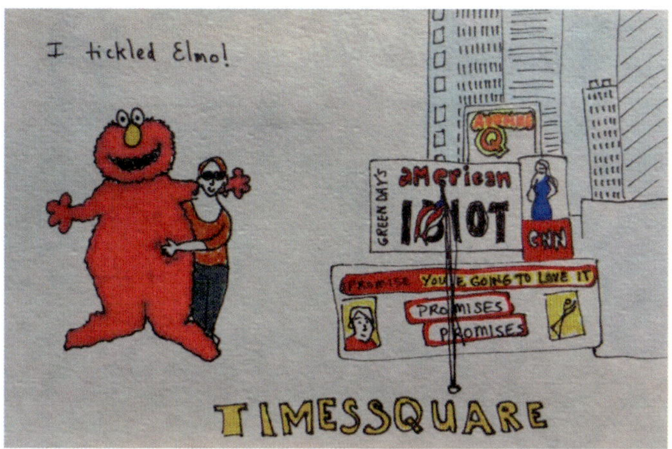

Fig.45

The ghost of King Kong can almost be seen, still swatting away airplanes as he scales the Empire State Building with Fay Wray in hand. Why didn't I draw that? Hmm.

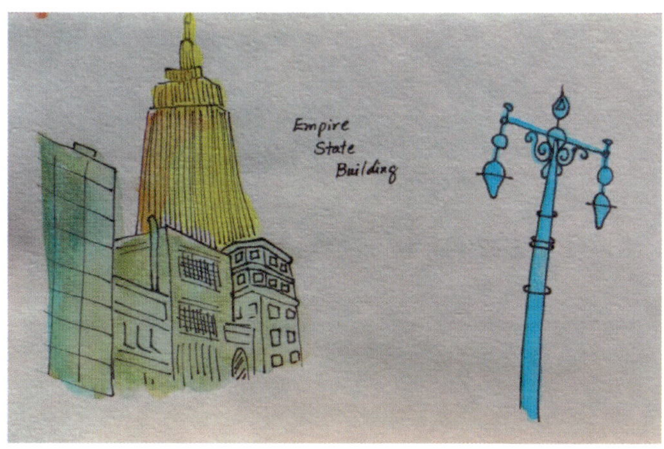

Fig.46

Thanks to Tracey, we were able to get tickets to a taping of The Colbert Report. I caught one of the Wrist Strong bands that Stephen shot into the studio audience, and it can be seen happily hugging the front cover of my journal.

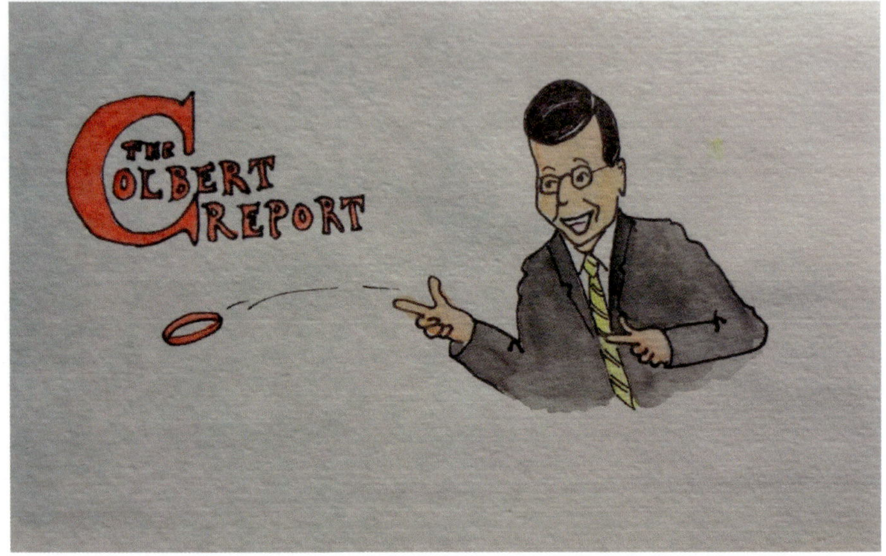

Fig.47

NOTE: Stephen, in case you're reading this, I love you! And no, this is **not** how you look to me. (Please refer to my earlier comments about drawing faces and laughing.)

MY CRAZIEST NEW YORK MOMENT: One evening, Tracey's friend JoAnne joined us at a lovely, quiet restaurant (which shall remain nameless) with white linen tablecloths and white pillars—very elegant. In stark contrast to all the white was a little black bug happily making loopty-loops on the wall by our table.

JoAnne exclaimed, *"I can't eat watching that cockroach crawl around. Tracey, kill it."* Sounded a bit like a mafia hit being ordered.

Tracey said, "*You know me, I don't kill bugs.*"

JoAnne looked at me since I was the next closest, and I said, "*I don't like to kill bugs either, but you can if you want.*"

JoAnne stood up, marched around the table, took off her shoe and slammed it against the wall, "*Thwack!*" echoing through the quiet restaurant. She put her shoe on, returned to her seat and said, "*Much better.*" She apparently was not disturbed in the least by the bloody mess on the wall. Yikes!

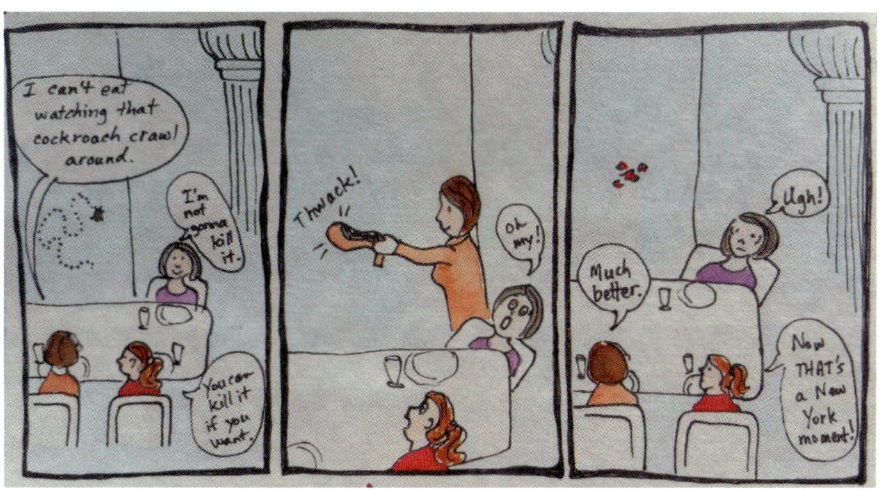

Fig.48

NOTE: This experience was so absurd to me that it seemed best expressed in a cartoon. Try drawing three or four frames and telling a story with your pictures to see what happens. If your journal opens flat, you might put two frames on one page and one or two more on the facing page. That would allow room to make your text a bit more legible.

One of my favorite sights was St. Patrick's cathedral with all its intricate details standing in sharp contrast to the sleek, modern buildings around it. It was truly spectacular.

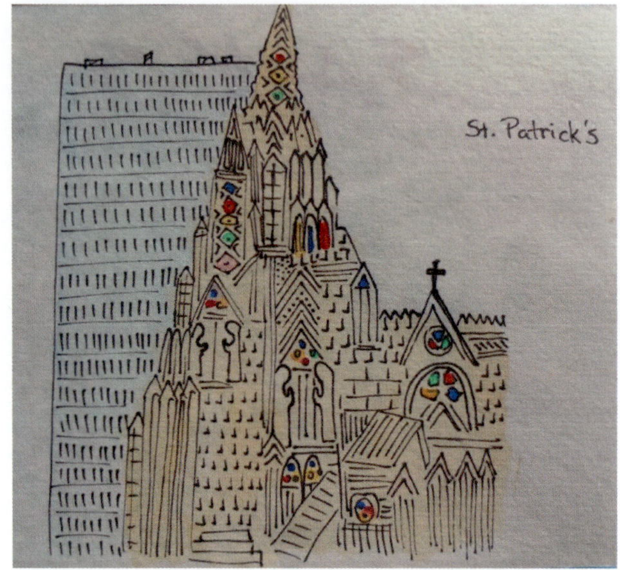

Fig.49

The fabulous shopping made me think of Eva Gabor: "Daaaahrling, I love you, but give me Park Avenue."

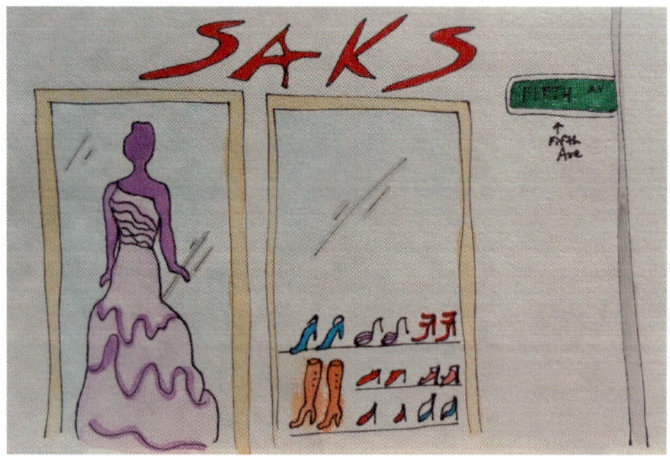

Fig.50

30 Rock. The plaza seemed so much bigger than on TV.

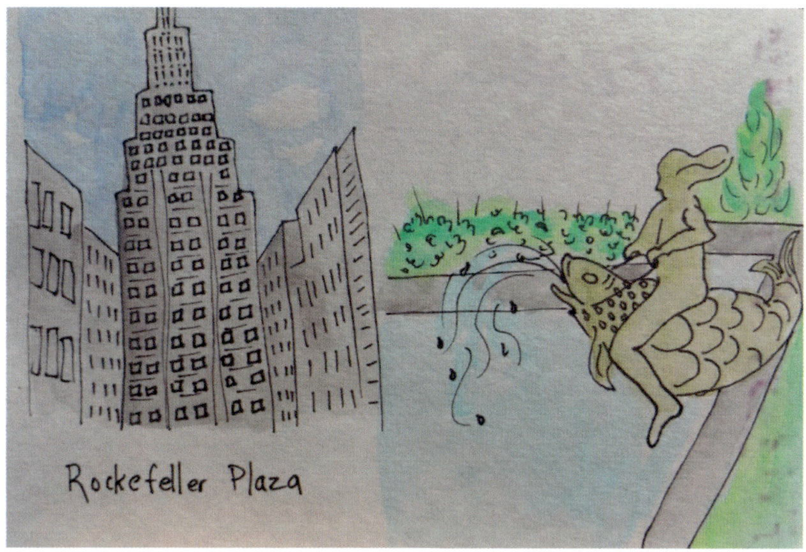

Fig.51

I enjoy taking double-decker bus tours when possible in any city I visit. The guides are usually entertaining and informative, and it gives a chance to rest my feet while still seeing the sights.

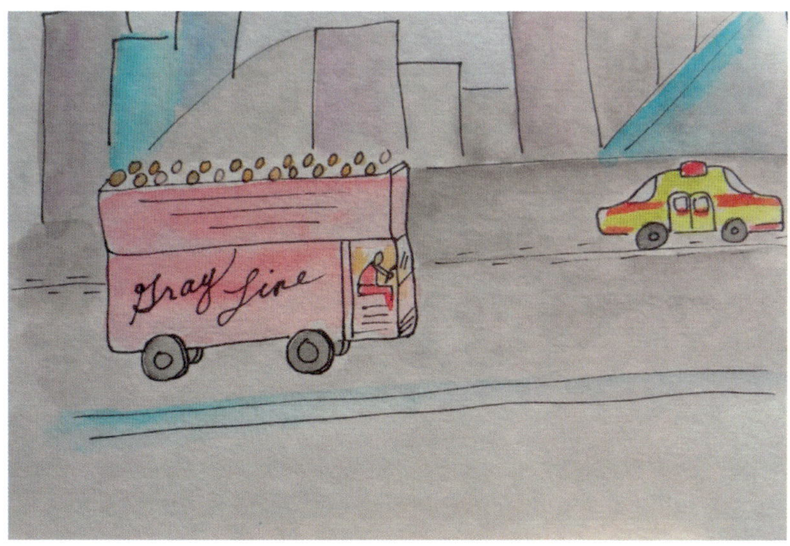

Fig.52

Battery Park was so beautiful and full of cultural significance. It has appeared in many movies, such as Sleepy Hollow, The Sorcerer's Apprentice, Men in Black 3, Desperately Seeking Susan, and has been mentioned in songs by Cole Porter, David Bowie, Bob Seger, John Mayer and so many more.

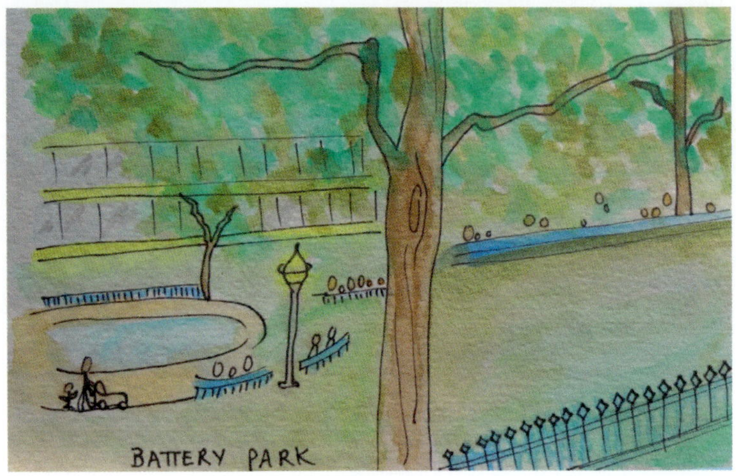

Fig.53

New York has such a variety of architectural styles side by side, some of which are painted in vibrant colors.

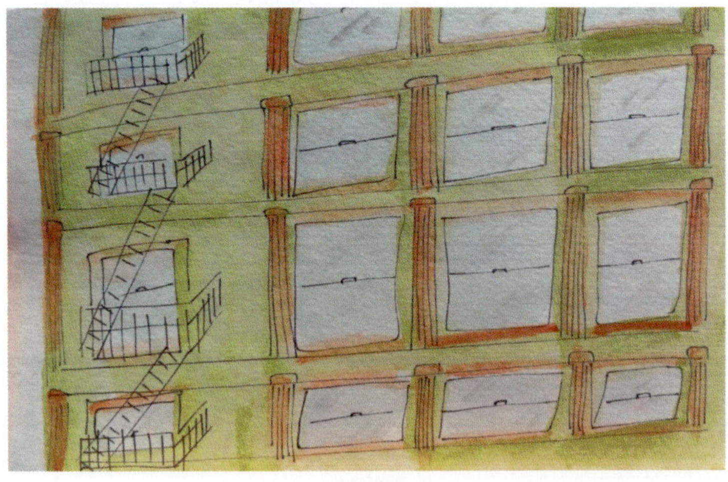

Fig.54

It is sad that the iconic Yaffa Café in the East Village is now closed. I'm glad I got to experience its eccentric décor and tasty treats.

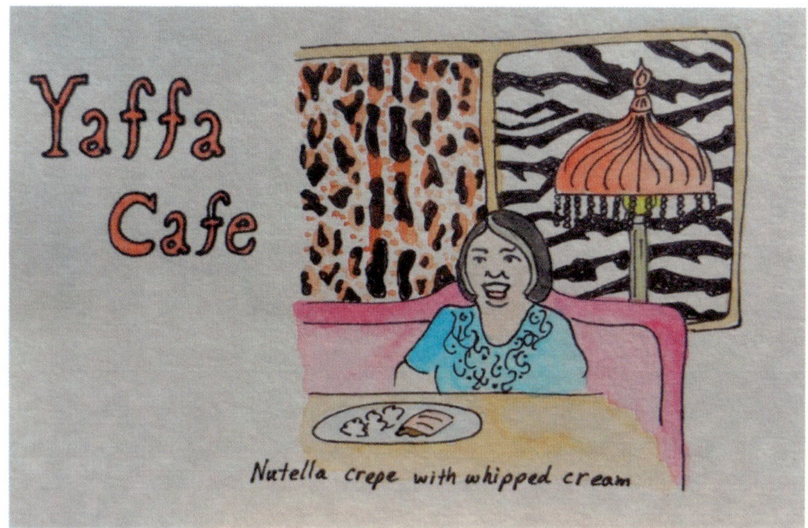

Fig.55

Next time I go to New York, I'll allow more time to just hang out in Central Park. Beautiful.

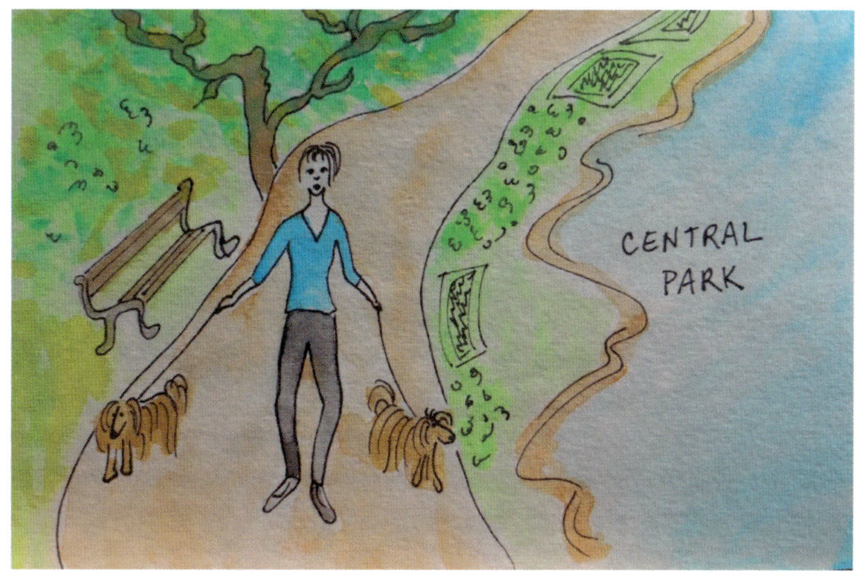

Fig.56

I ate my way through New York City (what a week!), and the Apple Jack Diner gets my vote for best cheesecake.

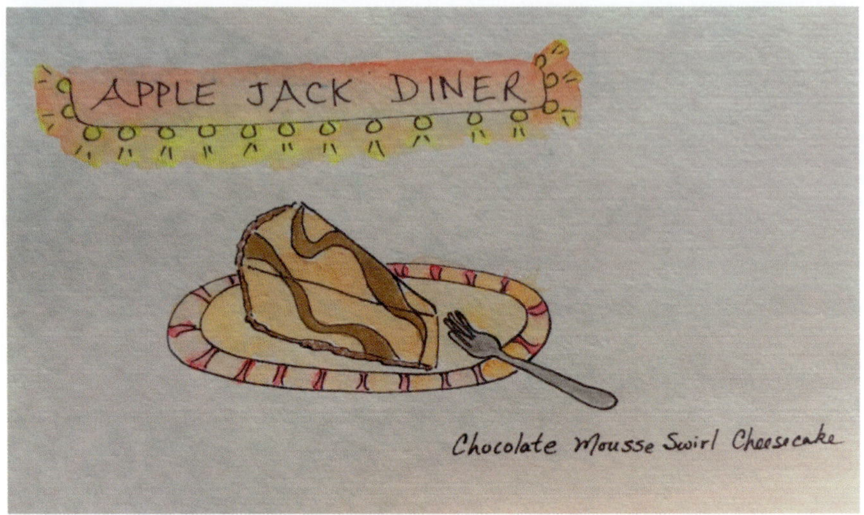

Fig.57

I never really noticed how unhappy the Statue of Liberty looked until I tried drawing her. She's very serious, indeed, but inspirational still.

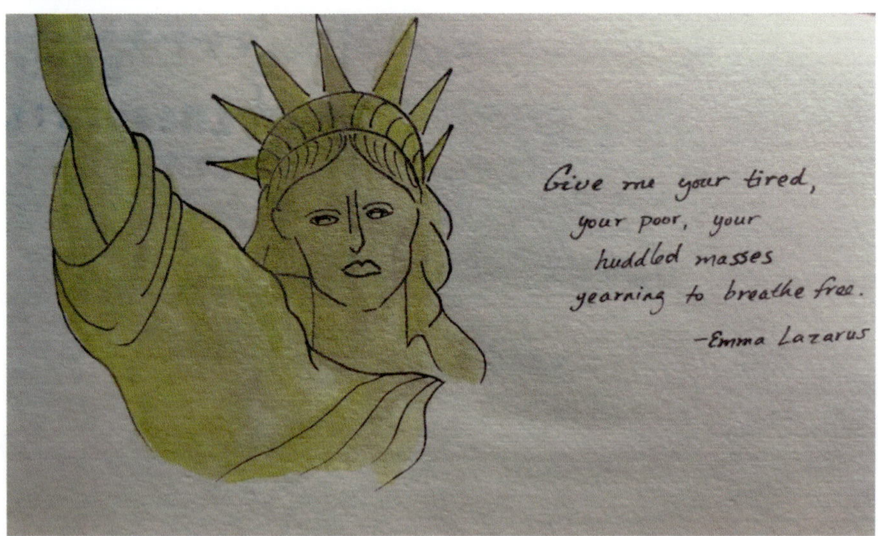

Fig.58

What trip to New York would be complete without seeing a Broadway show? Tracey and I went to see *Brief Encounter* at the Roundabout Theatre at Studio 54. I loved the romance and the special effects that made the characters step off the stage into a movie screen. Very cool. And the musical numbers were very sweet.

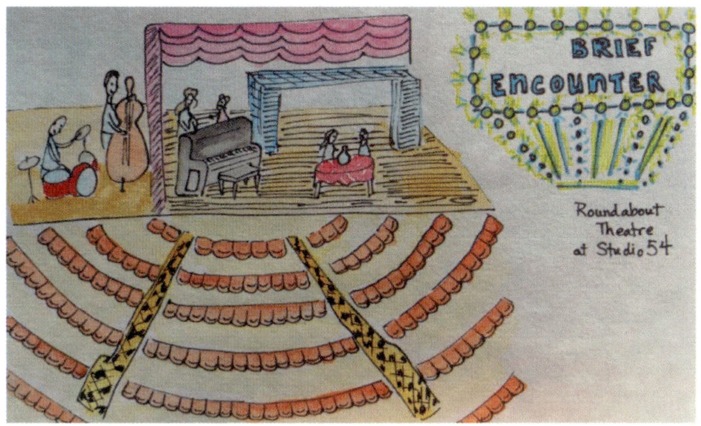

Fig.59

I wish I'd been able to see a performance at the Lincoln Center, but the building itself is beautiful.

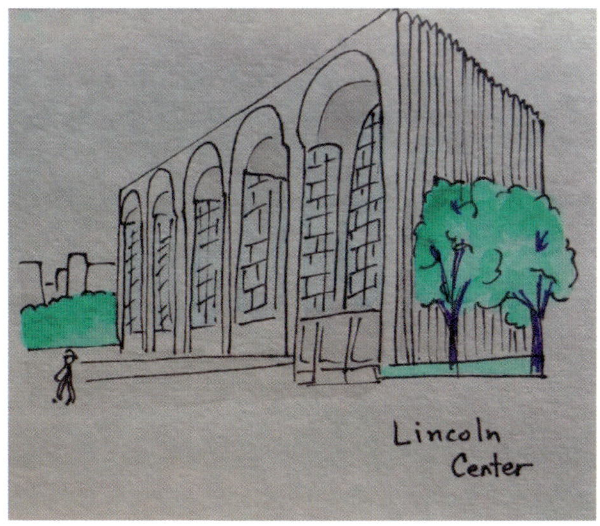

Fig.60

Here's the Magnolia Bakery sketch used in Chapter 3. It is a fabulous bakery with so many wonderful treats that were a delight just to see and smell. More delightful still to taste, of course.

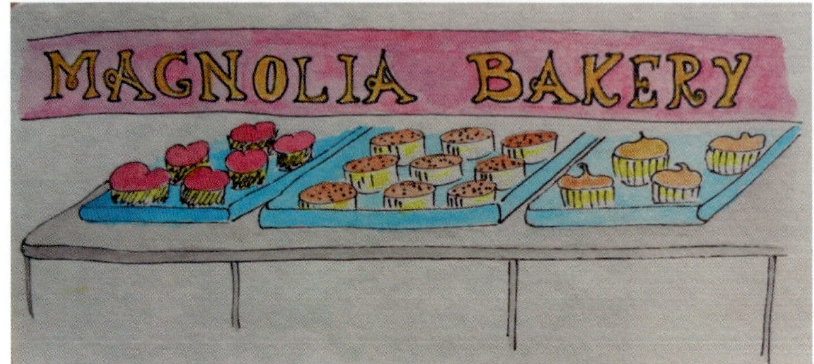

Fig.61

Never have I waited in line so long for a hamburger and enjoyed it so much! Yuuuuummyyyy!

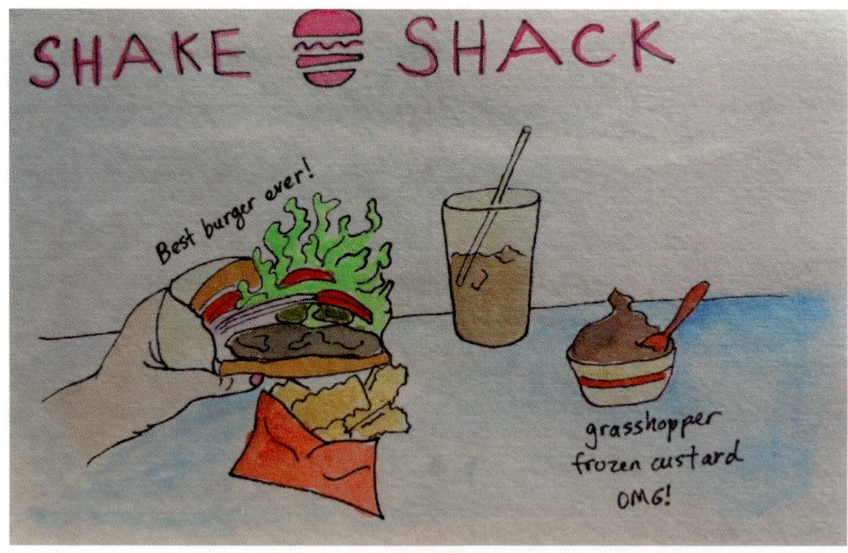

Fig.62

Grand Central Station was grand indeed!

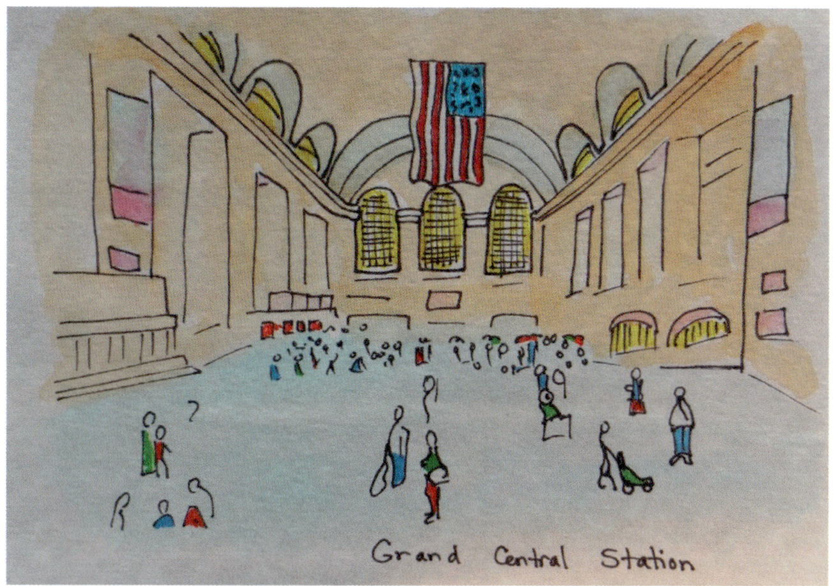

Fig.63

Beautiful 25-foot statue to one of my favorite composers.

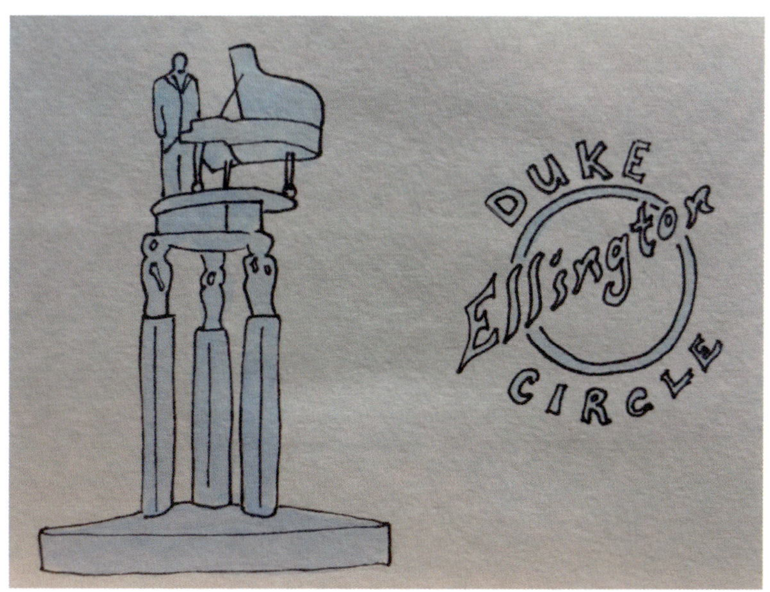

Fig.64

My metro card was my friend. It took me everywhere I wanted to go in New York via the subway.

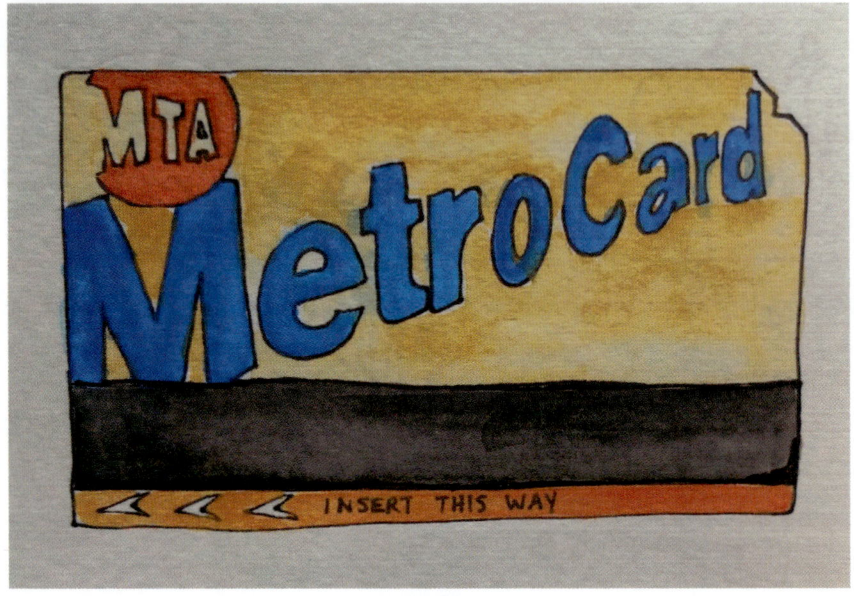

Fig.65

The watercolor sketches from my trip filled about half of the journal, so I used the remaining pages as a scrapbook for photographs. Here are a few of my favorite photo pages. While I enjoy looking at the photos, the watercolor pictures bring back richer memories of the magical moments in New York.

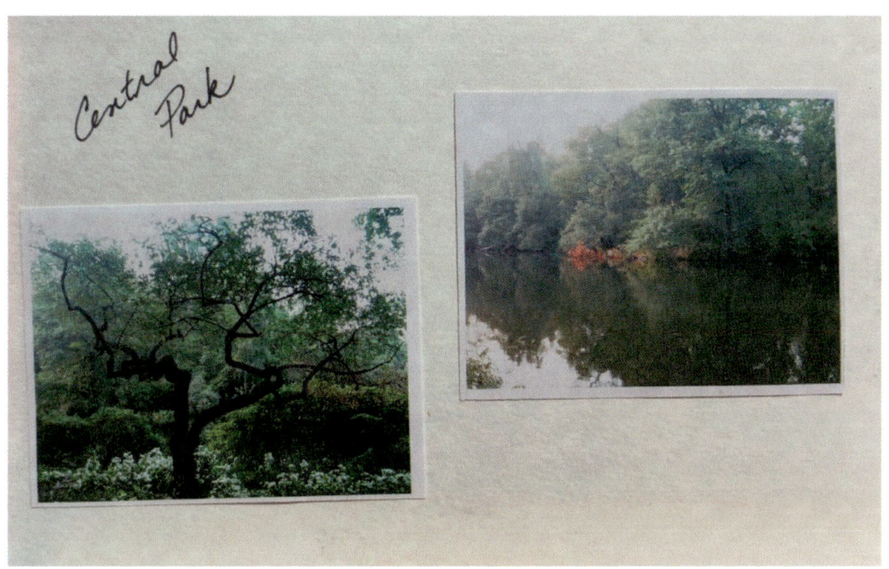

Fig.66

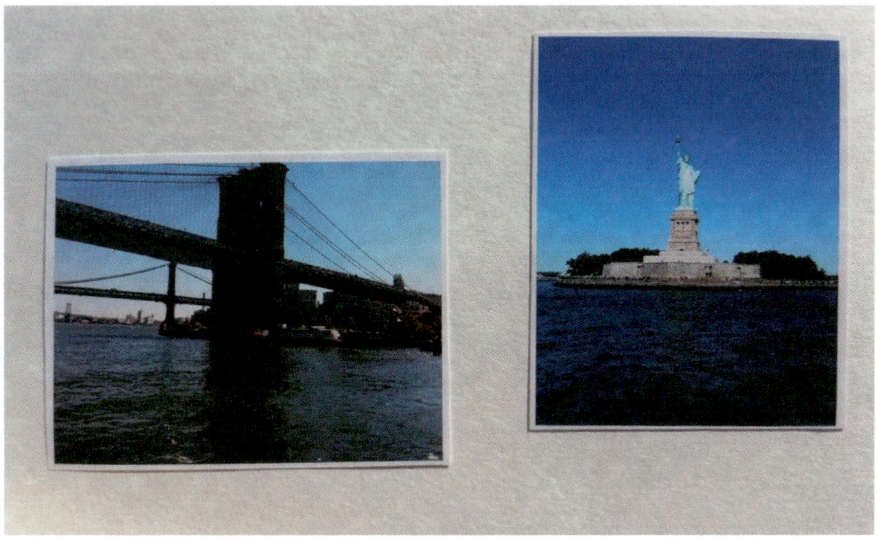

Fig.67

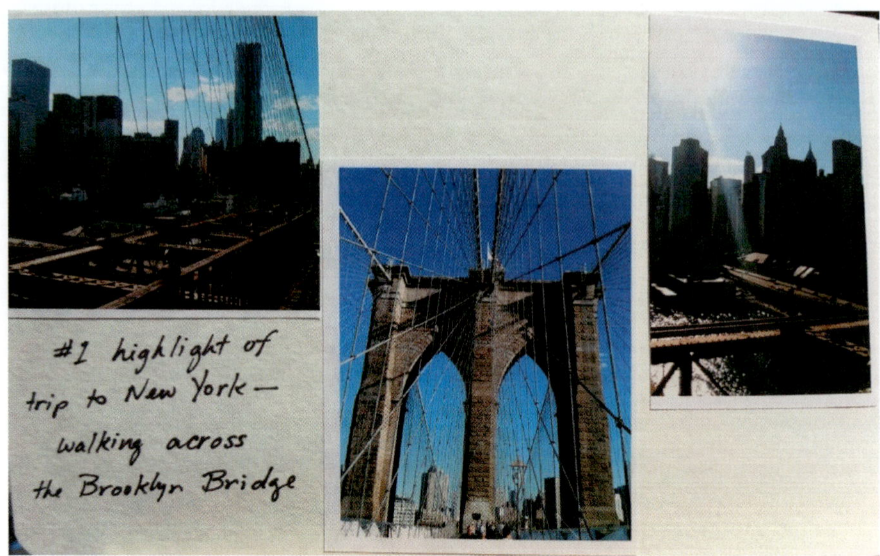
#1 highlight of
trip to New York —
walking across
the Brooklyn Bridge

Fig.68

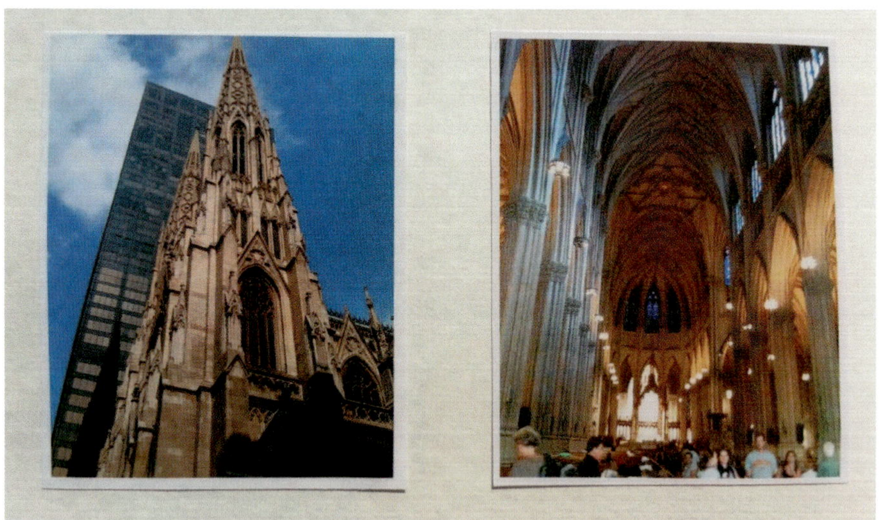

Fig.69

AT LOMBARDI'S
Scott's
Pizza
Tour
↑
Scott
↑
the slide test

Fig.70

OVER 100 YEARS
ALLEVA
VA - MOZZAREL
BEST QUALI
↑
Bob

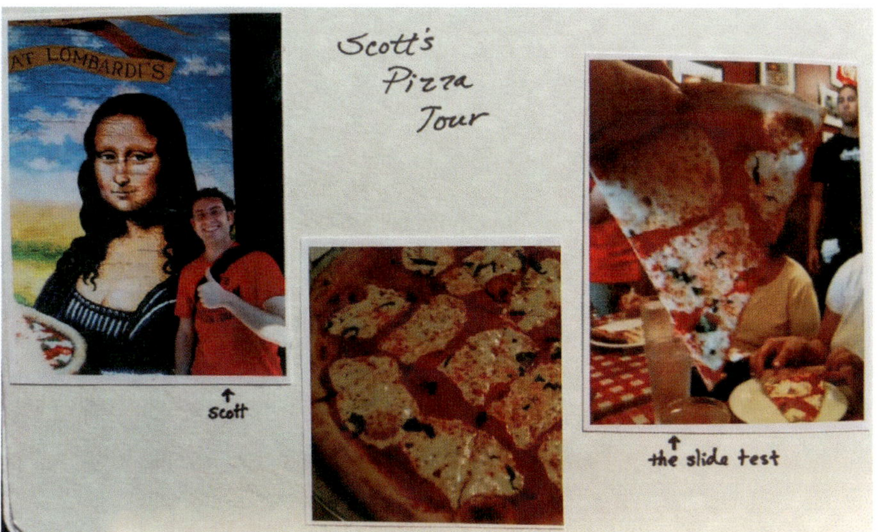

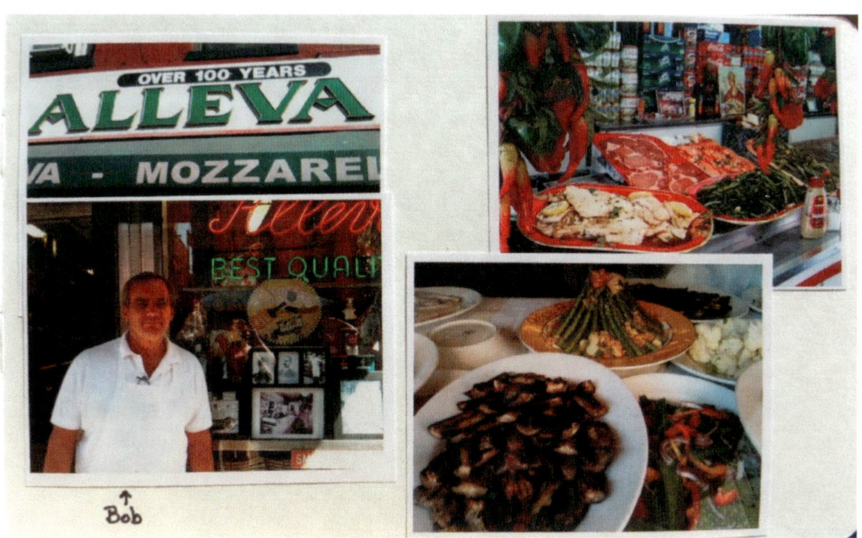

Fig.71

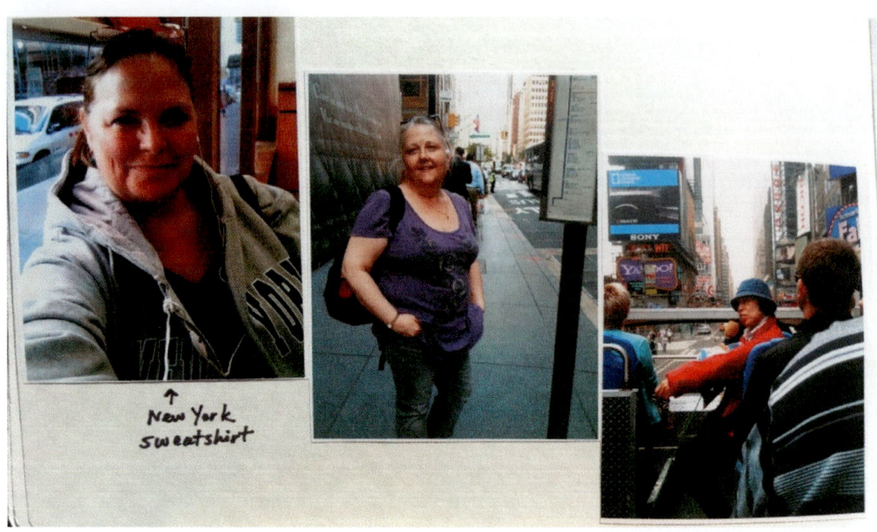

The "real" Tracey (center).

Fig.72

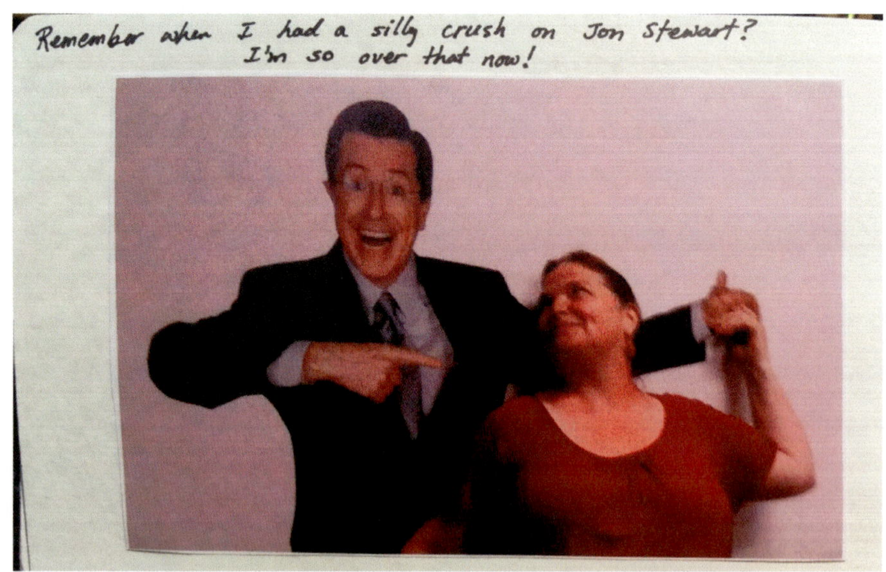

Fig.73

CHAPTER 7

THE SPICE OF LIFE

Don't know about you, but I become bored very quickly doing the same thing again and again. Following are simple techniques that can add variety to your painting.

ARTIST TAPE. Apply tape around the edges of your page, paint your picture, then carefully remove the tape to create a clean frame around the edges. I suggest using artist tape or yellow masking tape since the blue and green painter's tapes are not as forgiving on paper as they are on walls and are more likely to tear the page.

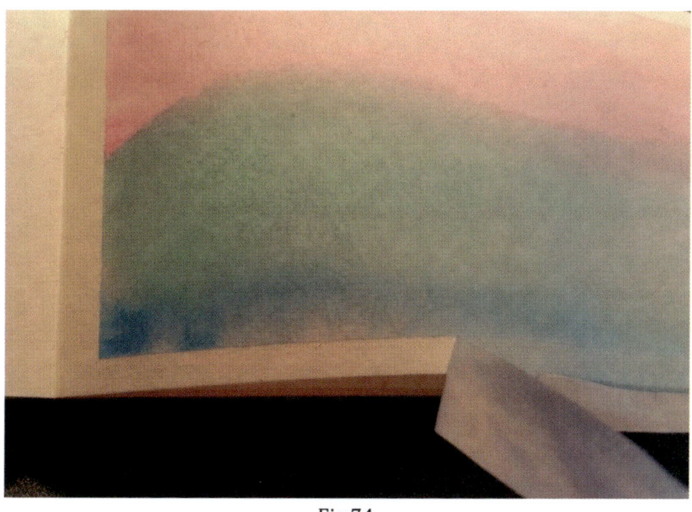

Fig.74

STENCILS & DIE CUTS. Lay a pre-cut stencil or a shape over your paper before painting, or maybe before adding a second layer of paint. Tapping with a stiff brush and using barely wet paint (not runny) works best for stencils.

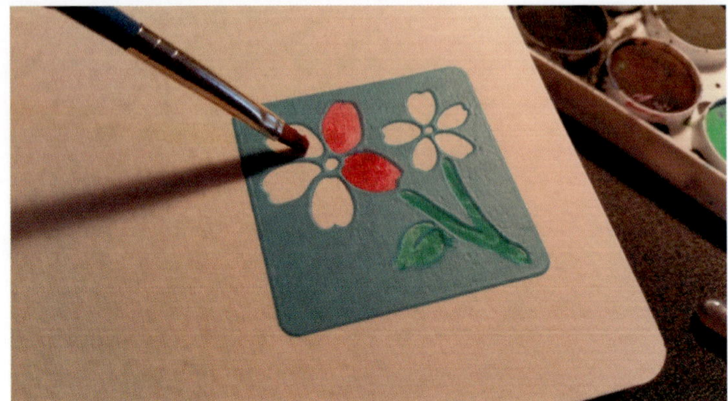
Fig.75

TISSUE PAPER. Wad up a tissue or paper towel to dab on wet paint. It will absorb the paint leaving white space to create shapes such as clouds.

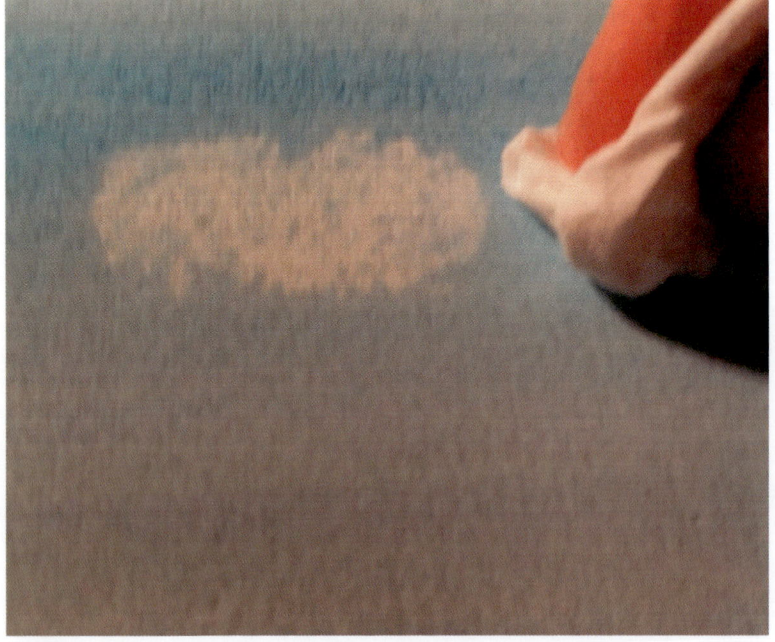
Fig.76

Twisting the tissue and laying it on your wet paint is an easy way to create waves.

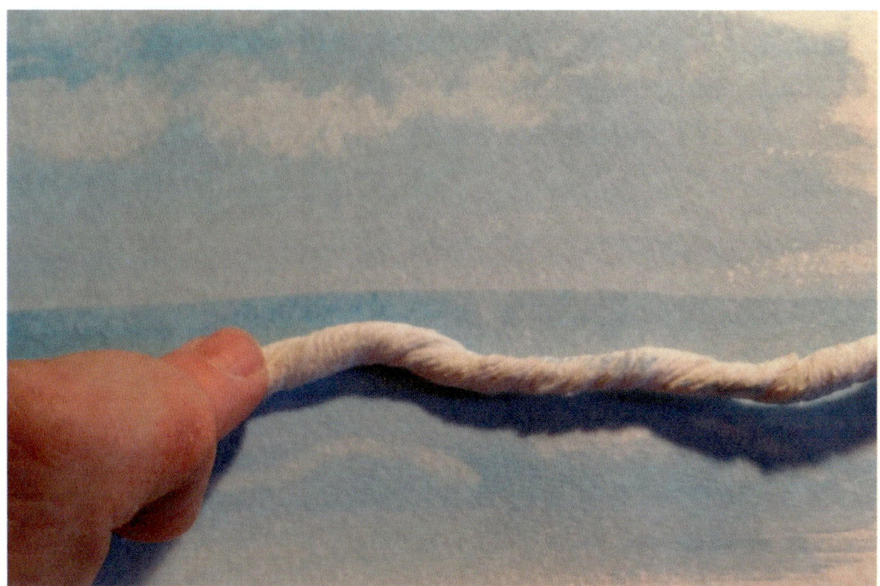

Fig.77

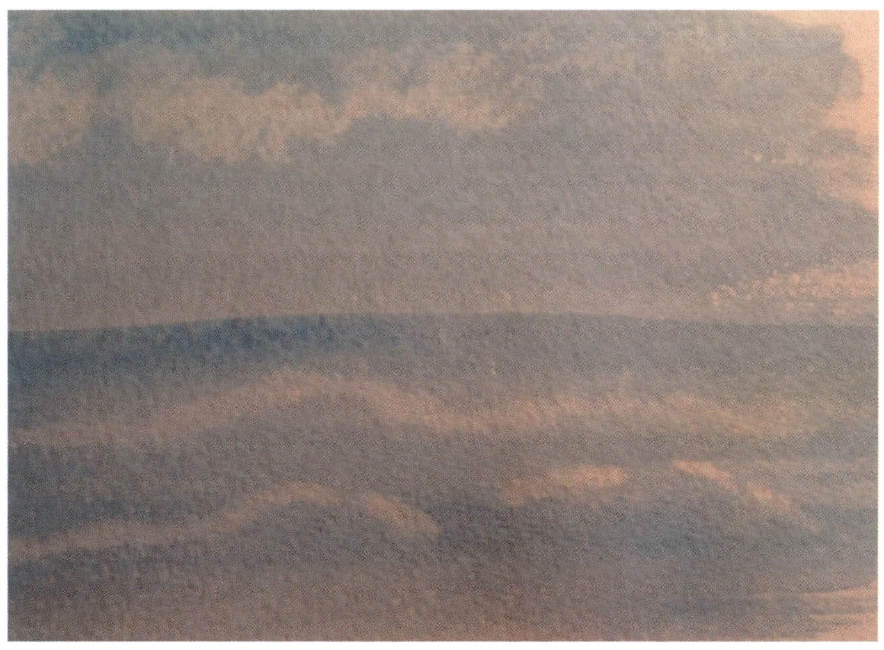

Fig.78

 Drizzle rubber cement on watercolor paper to create a design. Once the glue is completely dry, paint over it and let the paint dry well. Then carefully rub off the rubber cement to reveal your design. There are products such as Maskit which allow for better control for drawing or writing, instead of randomly drizzling.

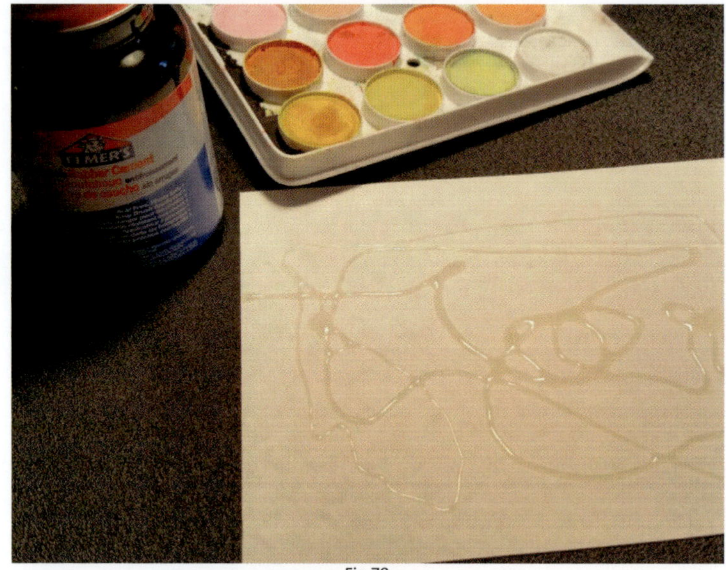

Fig.79

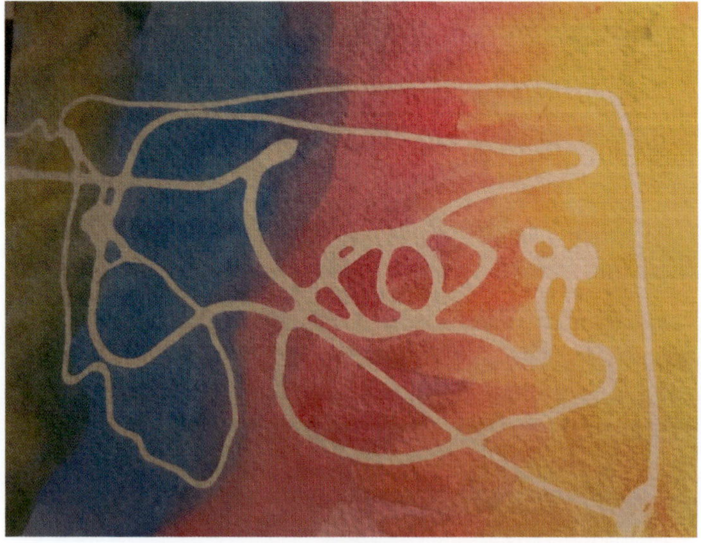

Fig.80

SALT. Sprinkle a pinch or two of salt over wet watercolor. It will soak up some of the water and leave a crackled texture. Once the paint has dried, brush off the salt.

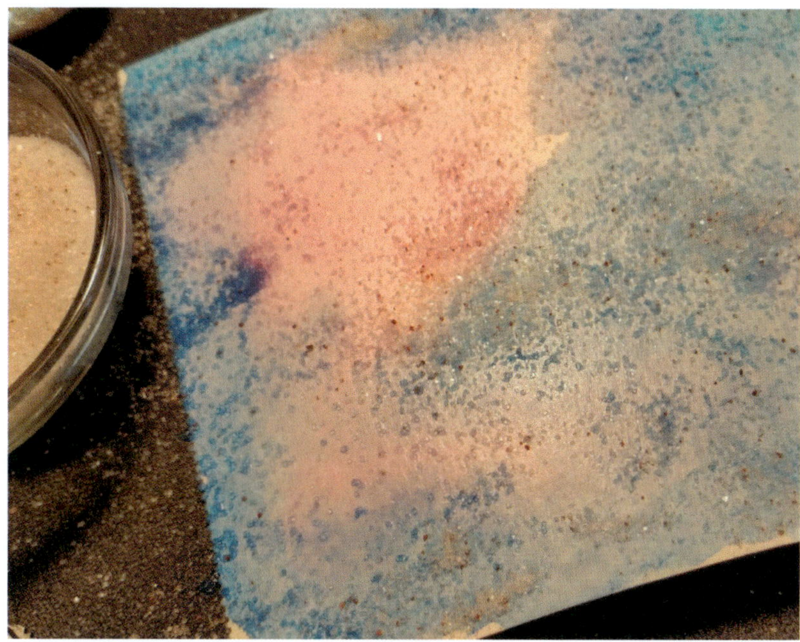
Fig.81

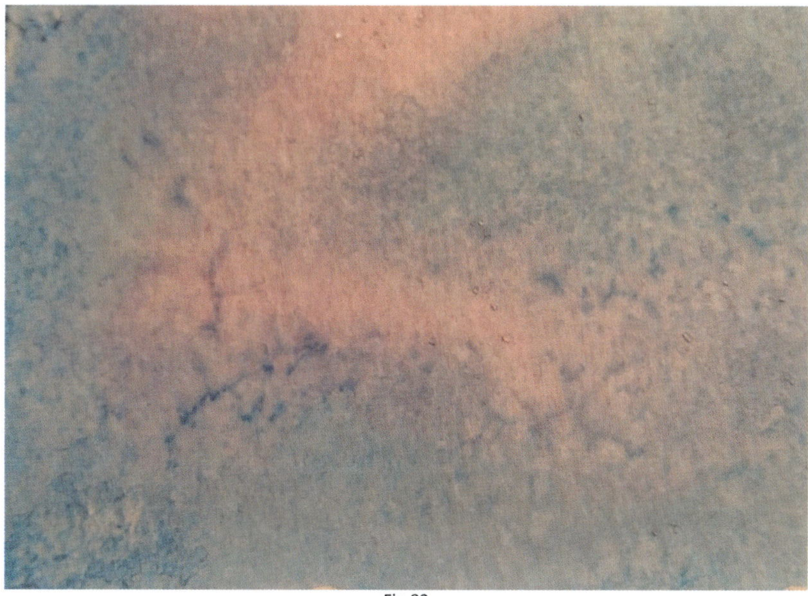
Fig.82

SPLATTERING. I like to use an old toothbrush to create a speckled effect. Dip the brush in the watercolor paint, hold it over your paper and use your finger to pull the bristles back. The wetter the paint, the larger the splatters. Be prepared for a mess, though, since the direction and distance of the splatters can be unpredictable until you've done it a few times.

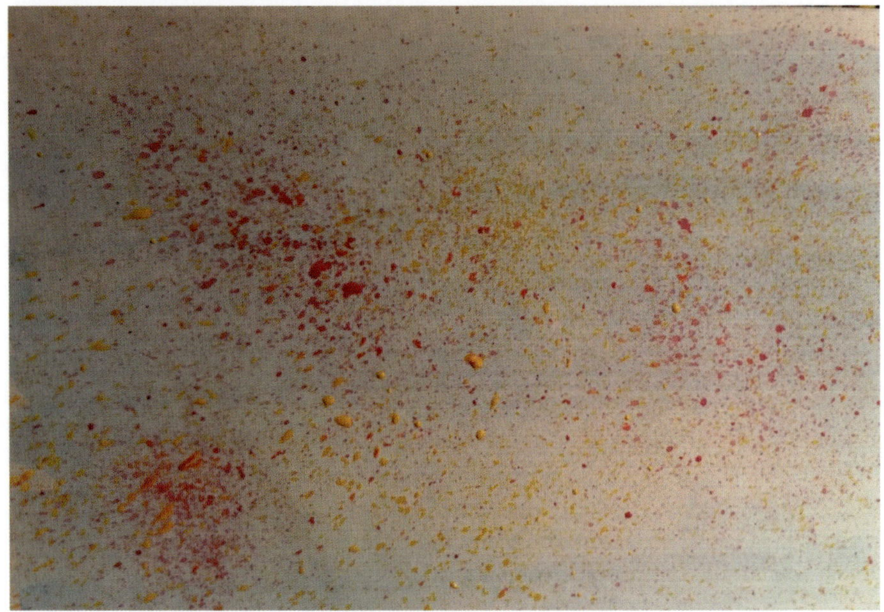
Fig.83

RUBBING ALCOHOL (ISOPROPYL). An interesting effect can be made by sprinkling drops of rubbing alcohol onto wet watercolor. It pushes the paint away and creates a spotted effect. It won't work once the watercolor is dry, so you have to work quickly. You can use an eye dropper, or even splatter it on with a toothbrush.

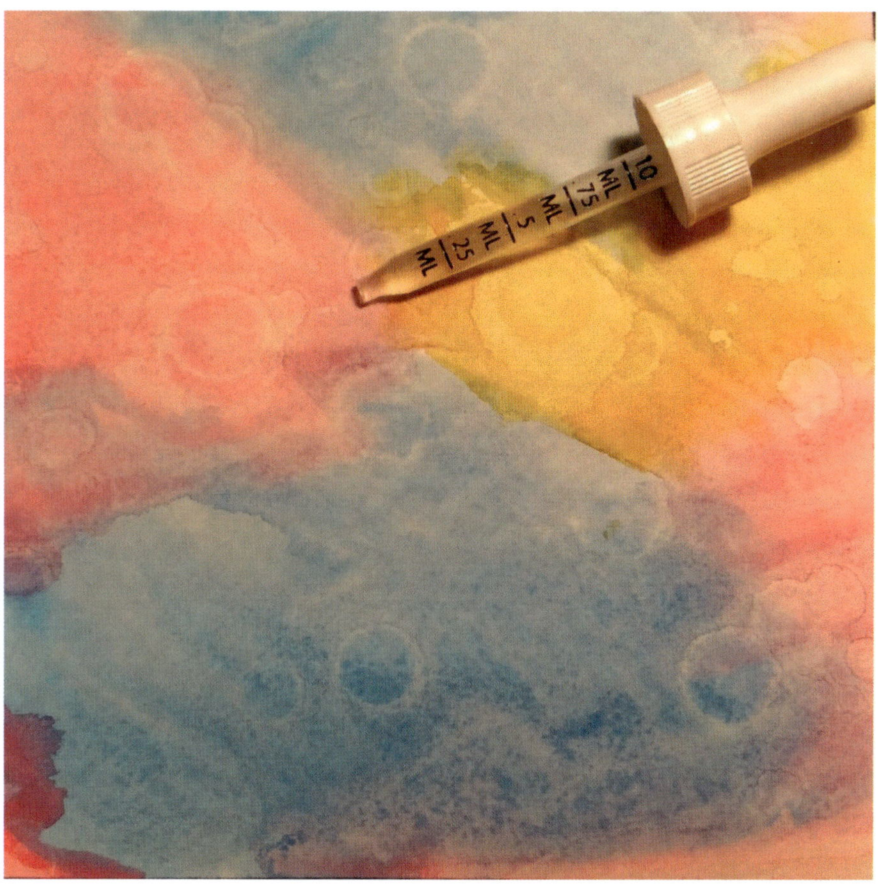

Fig.84

 Let your watercolor paint dry well and then paint over it. Each subsequent layer will get darker and add richness and texture. This painting is a copy of the program cover for a particularly steamy Zumanity performance. I painted the background red and added more red squiggles with each layer of paint until it actually began to look almost velvety. What a surprise that was! Just experiment. Your paintings will take on a life of their own.

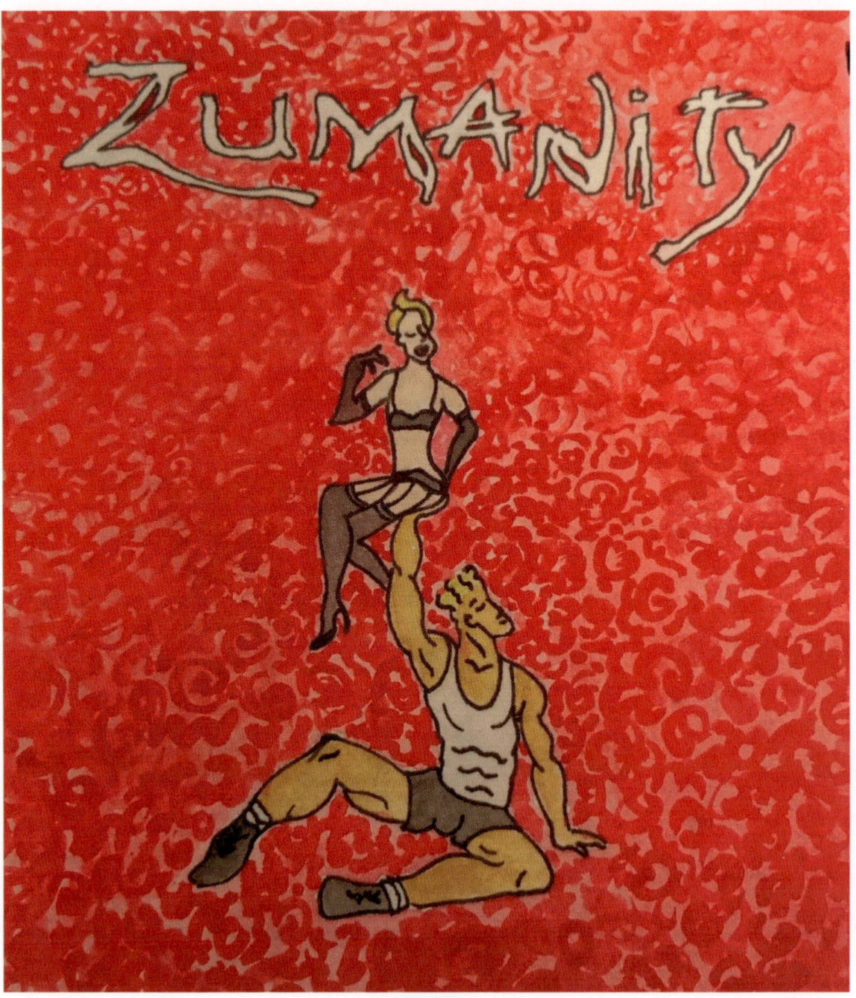

Fig.85

CHAPTER 8

GO FOR IT!

Ready or not, let's go! If you haven't put pencil to paper yet, now's the time. To quote Nike: **Just do it.** Remember that you don't ever have to show your art to anyone if you don't want to. Many a sketch or painting I've done has been ripped into shreds and thrown away quickly to hide the evidence. Matters not. Try, try again. I promise you, if you stick with it, there will come a moment when you create something that you simply can't believe you did, and that is such an amazing feeling.

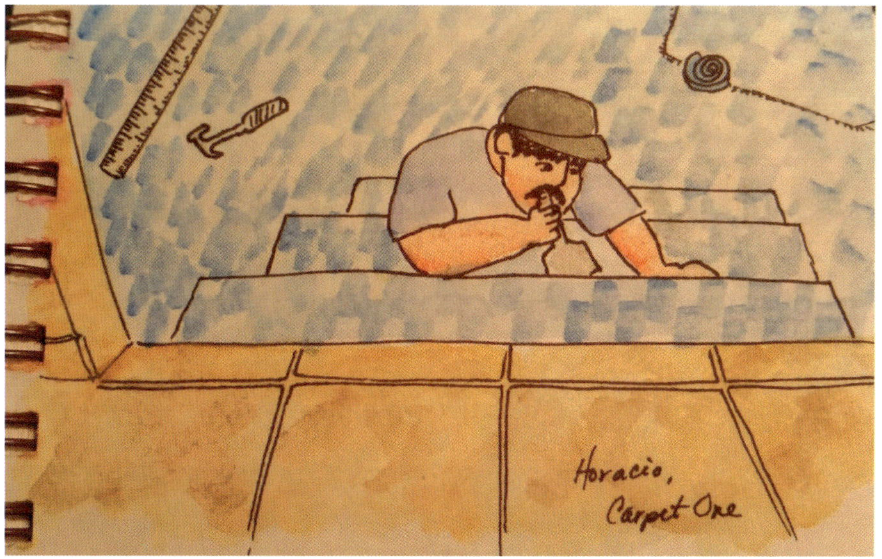

Fig.86

Please email me to let me know how it's going, to ask questions you may have, and to send pictures of any of your art that you are willing to share with me.

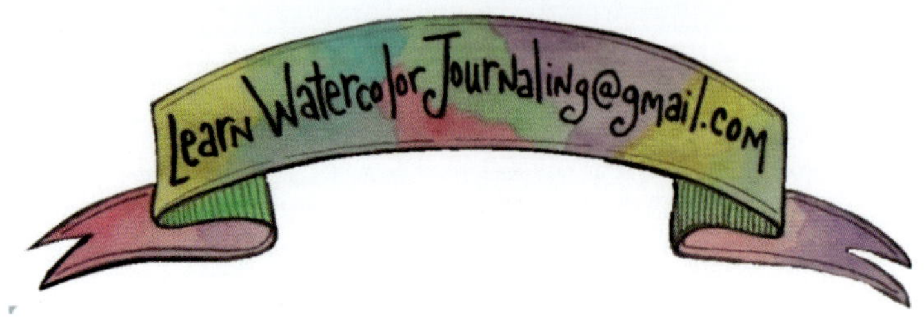

Fig.87

Here's what you'll get for taking the time to send me an email mentioning this book:

❶ **A CHANCE TO WIN** a complete watercolor journaling kit (as described in Chapter 2) valued at $50. Your email must be received ***by December 1, 2015*** to be included in the drawing. If you are reading this book after that date, please email anyway, because there may be future drawings.

❷ **A PERSONAL REPLY FROM ME**, including answers to any questions you may ask in your email. Hopefully I will receive an outrageous number of emails and, if so, it may take a bit of time for me to respond to you, but I will.

❸ **A LIST OF 100 IDEAS** of things to draw when you can't think of something on your own.

∂ ∂ ∂

Thank you for reading this book. I hope you have enjoyed it and that it has given you some ideas and helpful information for experiencing the joy of watercolor journaling. And now, the final call to action:

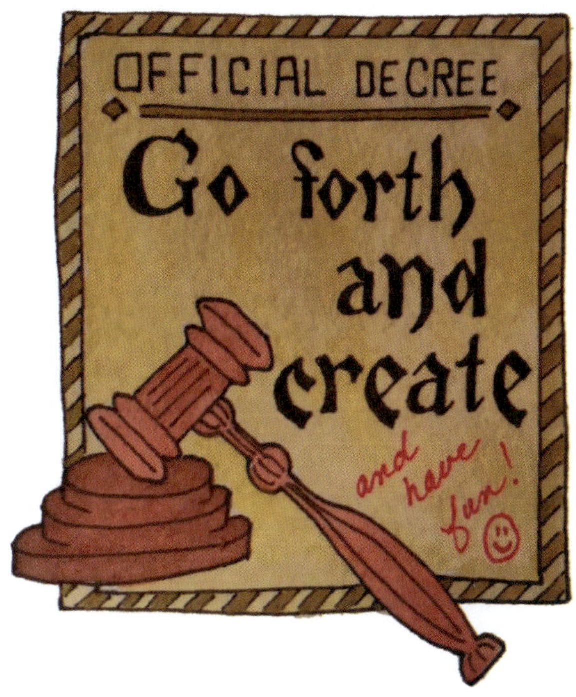

Fig.88

REQEST FOR REVIEWS

This is the first book I have published, so I would appreciate your feedback on how I can improve future editions of this book, or your advice for other books I intend to publish. Please email that to me, but remember I'm the sensitive, creative type with a very strong inner critic, so be honest, but gentle.

If you have enjoyed reading this book, I would greatly appreciate your writing a review on Amazon.com! Thank you!

REFERENCES

Hungry for more? There are so many resources available (many of them free!) to give you ideas and directions on how to improve your art or take it in a whole new direction. Here are just a few of my favorite art instruction YouTube tutorials, books and websites.

YouTube Tutorials:

Watercolor Painting Charleston, Rainbow Row:
https://www.youtube.com/watch?v=Yn9nYunUcjo
{Watch ANYTHING by Jennifer Branch—she's my favorite for watercoloring tutorials}

Drawing Exercises:
https://youtu.be/S1sW99idvak

Drawing Basics for the Clueless:
https://youtu.be/BFXvKpMfpEg

How to Draw Anything:
https://youtu.be/CqeuQF1qpvQ

Doodling: How to get started:
https://youtu.be/HRz5ZFDO0hk

Watercolor 101:
https://youtu.be/swMx54iFhLU

Watercolor Quick Tips and Tricks:
https://youtu.be/3_to3G-2mzI

Watercolor Starry Night Sky Demonstration:
https://youtu.be/0ebVULQPc-s

Watercolor Envelopes:
https://youtu.be/_sbTQotg0S4

Watercolor Burst Card - Start-To-Finish #27:
https://youtu.be/J3u7ULk-jQk

Watercolor Sketching & Journaling - Gay Kraeger:
https://www.youtube.com/watch?v=ozgcxLRwNtI

How to Illustrate a Stone Surface: Watercolor + Toothbrush!:
https://youtu.be/rmfIpXGes3I

Art Journaling Mixed Media: Break Free:
https://youtu.be/FG2njusqcEA

Art Journal Page:
https://youtu.be/QtVBV86nEb4

Art Journal Layout: Being Creative:
https://www.youtube.com/watch?v=5lMhSBbXxL0 *{Watch ANYTHING by Vicki Papaioannou—she's my favorite for mixed media art journaling tutorials}*

Books:

No Excuses Watercolor: Painting Techniques for Sketching and Journaling by Gina Rossi Armfield

Ideas & Inspirations for Art Journals & Sketchbooks by Suzanne McNeill

Keeping a Watercolor Sketch Book by Brenda Swenson

Discover Your World in Pen, Ink & Watercolor by Claudia Nice

Water Paper Paint: Exploring Creativity with Watercolor and Mixed Media by Heather Smith Jones

The Watercolor Journaling Handbook Spiral-bound by Tricia Reichert

ENDNOTES

27585029R00054

Printed in Great Britain
by Amazon